D1466676

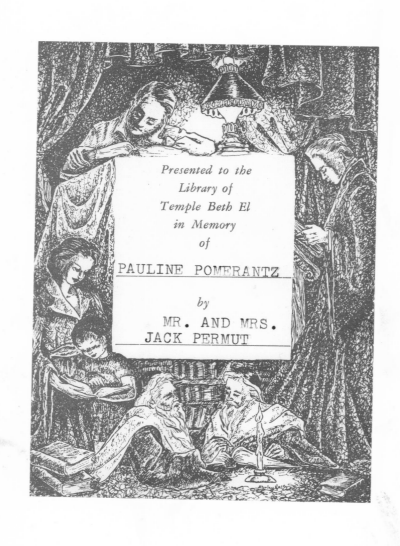

BETWEEN ENEMIES

By Amos Elon:

Journey through a Haunted Land
The Israelis: Founders and Sons

BETWEEN ENEMIES

A Compassionate Dialogue between an Israeli and an Arab

by AMOS ELON
and SANA HASSAN

RANDOM HOUSE 🏠 NEW YORK

Library of Congress Cataloging in Publication Data
Elon, Amos.
    Between enemies.
    1. Jewish-Arab relations.   I. Hassan, Sana.
II. Title.
DS119.7.E5   327.5694'017'4927   74-9077
ISBN 0-394-49514-4

Manufactured in the United States of America
9 8 7 6 5 4 3 2

First Edition

For Charlotte Leon Mayerson

who made this book possible, with
infinite patience and loving concern

Contents

1. How We Met—Who We Are, 3

2. Israel, 8

3. Israel and Egypt, 38

4. Israel and Syria, 80

5. Growing Up in Cairo—Growing Up in Tel Aviv, 96

6. The Palestinians, 115

7. The Distant Future, 144

BETWEEN ENEMIES

. . . the discovery of the reconciling formula is always
left to future generations in which passions have cooled
into curiosity and agonies of peoples have become the
exercise in the schools. The devil who builds bridges
does not span such chasms till much that is precious to
mankind has vanished down them for ever.

—R. H. TAWNEY

1

How We Met-Who We Are

Elon: Isn't it amazing, Sana, that after twenty-five years of bloodshed and terror, we find ourselves—an Arab and an Israeli—engaged in a public dialogue? Even now we live in what still seems only a temporary lull in the hostilities. Here we are, and yet, isn't it odd that we have to converse in English? That neither of us speaks the other's language is really a shame, and sad. Why have such dialogues been impossible so far?

Hassan: I think it was a terrible and tragic mistake on the part of us Arabs not to talk to you Israelis before. We need such dialogues. Without them, any peace settlement will be just a scrap of paper. We have to break through the prejudices and stereotypes which keep us apart, and peel away at the layers of accumulated hatred which are between us. I think that we Arabs never agreed to talk to you before because we felt it would be granting Israel a kind of moral legitimacy. This we were unprepared to do.

Elon: And are you now?

Hassan: Even now, probably, most Arabs would be unprepared to talk. They still think of peace more in negative terms, as an absence of war rather than as a positive thing, as interaction, as sharing. They do not see that the establishment of diplomatic relations, cultural exchanges, tourism, commerce, and so forth, are bound to follow. But this will inevitably come. This takes time and we all have to be patient. We must first of all start with a formal peace in order to be able to reach a real peace later on.

Elon: But when? But how?

Hassan: Above all, we must talk to each other. Our hostility has been autistic. We have not even reached the most basic level of human communication. We haven't even found a way to explain to each other our aggravation, our rage. If we could only achieve that much communication, then there would be some ground for hope.

It's incredible that our countries know absolutely nothing about each other. There have been people before that fought protracted wars, like the Germans and the French, for example, but at least they spoke to each other, they traveled in each other's countries, they read each other's literature. We live in total ignorance of each other. We are trapped in clichés and stereotypes. When we see Israelis in the street, it is almost like watching creatures from Mars. We are almost surprised that they have eyes or noses or feet. We find their living reality extraordinary. Although we know that Israel exists, we know it only in an abstract sense.

Elon: As you know, Sana, most peoples are ignorant of each other. That's not so unusual even among people who live in peace. I don't know how many stereotyped notions Americans and Mexicans have of each other, Americans of Russians, Frenchmen of Germans, but I suspect that there are many. Schopenhauer said that every nation derides the other and that all are right . . . that sardonic attitude may be a good antidote to nationalism; but in our case we have gone too far. The extraordinary, even unique feature of our conflict, a feature which makes one almost despair, is that there's a total lack of contact not only between the peoples, but what's worse, between our governments as well. Our leaders have never met, our diplomats have never talked, they've never had the opportunity to get to know one another, to become familiar with the fears, the hopes, the passions that make them tick as political leaders and as human beings. This has never happened elsewhere and perhaps this is why our conflict seems so different, so tragic and so difficult to resolve. Even as individuals, we never seem to get together, except as potential killers or victims.

Hassan: Well, I'm glad we met.

Elon: I can't begin to tell you how glad I am. Even that,

Sana, was an accident which could easily not have happened at all. I arrived in America early in March to give a series of lectures on behalf of the United Jewish Appeal's Israel Emergency Fund. I am too old to serve in an Israeli army combat unit, and when the last war was over, I felt that next to driving a truck or an ambulance, the best I could do for Israel was to help raise funds, and to help get Israel's case across to American college audiences. On the second day here, quite by accident, I saw an article you had written a few weeks earlier in the *New York Times Magazine*. I was astounded by this article, in which you pleaded not only for peace but also said that Israel's moral case was as good as the moral case of the Arab. You recognized Israel's historic rights. As far as I know, no Arab had ever made such an admission before, at least not in public. I mentioned your article as a hopeful sign in a lecture I gave in Harvard Hall. I didn't know at the time that you were in the audience.

Hassan: I went to that lecture because I was curious to see you. I am a Ph.D. candidate at Harvard University in political science, but I travel back and forth to Egypt all the time. My specialty is Middle Eastern politics and I guess my interest in this subject derives also from the fact that my father is a former Egyptian ambassador and Cabinet minister, and that I'm married to a high Egyptian government official. I read your book *The Israelis: Founders and Sons* three years ago and I was as astounded by it as you were by my article. It was one of the very few books which helped me discover the other face of Israel which we Arabs never see—the more humane and decent face. The usual way we get to see you is in uniform, and that's hardly conducive to helping us understand you.

With your book, I felt that you, more than any Israeli I've ever encountered, had an extraordinary ability to understand our fears and anxieties and to recognize our rights without compromising your own. You showed an empathy that really moved me, all the more so because your love for Israel, which came through very strongly throughout the book, was not self-righteous and sanctimonious but understanding and critical. This for me was almost infectious. For the first time in my life it made me feel capable of putting myself in the skin of an Israeli. I believe, as your book implied, that real love is the ability to accept the bad along with the good and to recognize it, to be able to weep for one's country as well as to applaud it.

And so, as I was sitting in the Harvard audience, I decided I had to get together with you and talk to you.

Elon: I can't tell you how excited I am that this opportunity to talk came about. But let me make a suggestion. In this dialogue, let us aim at more than just a discussion. Let's not try to score points. Rather, let us try to meet as two human beings equally enmeshed in an enormous tragedy and equally aware of it—if you like, in a mutual exercise of self-awareness.

Hassan: Yes, that is what I too would like, it's what we *need* to do.

2

Israel

Hassan: Amos, you're not the first Israeli I've ever met, but somehow I have never had this kind of human rapport with an Israeli before. I wonder why? I think it's because you personalize the conflict for me. All of a sudden it is no longer only politics, or armies against armies. I have always cared about casualties, not only on our side but on your side too. They matter to me, but for the first time, your casualties are more than just abstract statistics.

Elon: You are the first Egyptian I've really ever spoken to. Meeting them in war, as I've done too often in the army in the past, is not the same thing. When I lived in Washington for a couple of years in the 1960s, I made vain attempts to meet Egyptians privately. Once at a

party I was introduced to the Egyptian press attaché.
When he heard who I was, he refused to shake hands,
turned his back on me and walked away.

Hassan: That's the problem. We Arabs have never given
ourselves the chance to meet you outside of our stereotypes and our prejudices. My father was Egyptian ambassador to the United States in the forties, and it so happened that he was our delegate to the UN General
Assembly which decided on November 29, 1947, to establish the state of Israel. Of course, he fought this decision
vehemently. His opposite on the Israeli side was your
Foreign Minister Abba Eban. My father later told me
that Eban had sent him a message after one of the meet-
ings telling him that he would very much like to meet
him privately. My father refused, and here I am, his
daughter, one generation later, meeting you and talking
to you just down the street from the UN headquarters
on the East River, where Arabs and Israelis are still
fighting publicly and never meeting privately. I suspect
my father, twenty-seven years ago, intensely disliked
what he had to do for political propriety's sake. He is
retired now and is probably pleased that we are talking.

Elon: And yet, all Israelis cannot meet all Egyptians. So how
can we break these mental stereotypes, Sana? I feel that
both sides, you and I, you and we, are still fighting ghosts
of the past. The Arabs contend with the phantoms of
British and French imperialism, we with horrendous
shadows of our ghastly past. Behind every Arab soldier,
we see an S.S. man.

Hassan: I'm glad to say that quite a few Egyptians are themselves aware that they respond to stereotypes. When I was in Egypt last year, this joke was circulating: An Egyptian fellah returns to his village from the 1967 war. He boasts that he has just fought off a French invasion. His fellow peasants sneer at him. "What French invasion, you idiot? This is not the 1956 war. In this war there were only Israelis." "No, no," he protests. "I tell you, I was fighting the French." "How could you tell that they were French?" "Because they were tall, blond and decent, and the Israelis are short, dark, hunchbacked, with hooked noses, and they're horrible."

Elon: There are similar stereotypes on our side. In Israel we often go from one extreme to another. If we don't view you as monstrous Nazi devils, we tend to look at you as subhuman or irrelevant. The Hebrew colloquialism for a shoddy, sloppy job is *avoda aravit*—"Arab work." When you want to tell a man, "Don't be a fool," or "Don't be devious," you tell him, *"Al tehiye aravi"*— "Don't be an Arab."

Hassan: Isn't this because you are still governed by the same aged European establishment which has all the prejudices Europeans had in the first part of the twentieth century when they were still the colonial overlords of Africa and Asia?

Elon: No. On a popular level, the resentment of the Arab is not predominant among European Jews, but mostly among Jews who fled to Israel from the Arab countries.

Among the latter this feeling sometimes borders upon real hatred. This might seem a paradox, but that's how it is. Moreover, the East European establishment of which you speak was really *sui generis*. It never reflected the social prejudices of nineteenth-century or early-twentieth-century Europe. It revolted against them. It was a child of European humanism, not colonialism. It postulated freedom and justice, not prejudice, social or ethnic. The Zionists were motivated by two basic factors: one was memory, the memory of a lost homeland to be regained for a dispersed people, persecuted and down-trodden, and still without a territory of its own; the other was a desire to establish a just society, for Jews and for those Arabs who would live among them.

It is so important, Sana, to remember this background, for it has been your tragedy and ours that the original Zionist dream became so enmeshed in war that it was never fully realized. The original Zionist dream never envisaged the establishment of merely another ordinary nation-state. On the contrary, it was widely felt at the time—and to an extent, it's still felt now—that if the Jews are to take this unusual step, gathering in their exiles, if we make this marvelous leap against time, against precedent, even against so-called sane argument (Chaim Weizmann said, "You don't have to be crazy to be a Zionist, but it helps")—if we take this unusual step, it will have to be for something considerably better than just another nation-state. Theodor Herzl, the father of modern Zionism, envisaged an open society—as he put it, "a *Genossenschaft*," a free commonwealth. Weizmann said time and again, "Let's not create another Lithuania, or

Rumania, or Poland. There are enough of those already."
David Ben-Gurion went even further when he claimed
that Israel must be *"ner lagoyim,"* a light to the nations
of the earth, "a model for the redemption of the entire
human race." This was the ethos of that East European
establishment of which you speak.

Hassan: What you say really moves me, Amos. It is a very
beautiful dream, but what has become of it? Please do not
misunderstand me. I do not wish to sound cynical. Quite
the contrary, it is precisely because I too believe in the
dream that my disappointment is so great. I ceased to think
of Israelis as devils when I first read about men like
Chaim Weizmann or Martin Buber or Yehuda Magnes.
Long before I had the opportunity to meet Israelis in
flesh and blood, I was impressed by their Utopian ex-
pectations.

You cannot imagine the impact upon me of most
Israelis I've met so far. It was often quite shattering. To
be sure, Israelis did not turn out to be the ruthless villains depicted to me in my early childhood in Egypt,
but neither were they the noble creatures whom you have
just described. The trouble is that they were frequently,
I'm sorry to say, parochial, smug, petty, self-centered and
arrogant. They hardly took the trouble to disguise their
contempt for Arabs. It is ironic and sad that the Jews, who
were themselves the objects of scorn throughout their history, should now hold another nation in contempt. I should
think that Israelis would have enough national achievements to be proud of, without having to support their
pride with contempt for the Arabs. But perhaps this con-

tempt plays a compensatory role for the scorn they themselves experienced in the past, as well as the scorn Oriental
Jews now experience at the hands of Western Jews. Once,
when I was in Paris, I overheard a conversation between an
Israeli officer and an elderly French lady in the bus traveling from Le Bourget Airport to the Place des Invalides. He
was telling her of the burning of the Al Aksa Mosque in
Jerusalem, which had just taken place. He told her that he
was sure an Arab had done it just to cause trouble for
Israel.*

I could not resist the temptation, even though I did
not know him. I turned around and said in French, "You
must really hate the Arabs."

He answered, not knowing that I was an Egyptian, "No,
I have no feelings for them, one way or the other. I
neither love them nor hate them. They are animals, they
behave like animals, they live like animals, they think
like animals."

Perhaps this officer was not typical. Perhaps he was not
too sophisticated. But most of my experiences with Israelis
at Harvard, who I presume are the intellectual elite of
your country, have differed only in degree, not in kind.
They usually display either contempt for the Arab or
utter ignorance. Once, in a course I was taking on nationalism, I said that one of the problems of economic development in Egypt was that we overproduced engineers
whom we have to export to other Arab countries because
we cannot find jobs for them. An Israeli student sneer-
ingly replied, "What? You mean Egypt has engineers?"

* The arsonist was, in fact, a demented Australian tourist who claimed in
court, later on, that he had been acting under instructions from Jesus Christ.

Another time, an Israeli whom I met for the first time in a class on political theory asked me what university I had attended in Egypt. When I told him, he looked at me with utter surprise and said, "I did not know that you had any universities in Egypt other than Al Azhar University." I find it peculiar that an educated Israeli is so ignorant. Al Azhar is a religious university, a relic from the nineteenth century. Nowadays most Egyptian students attend other secular universities. There are five of them, with over two hundred and forty thousand students, while in Al Azhar there are only a few hundred students.

Elon: I wish you would go to Israel first and see for yourself before you make up your mind through chance encounters on a bus or the insensitive banter of some student. The guy you speak of may be a Harvard Ph.D. candidate, but that doesn't make him representative of the Israeli intellectual elite any more than the Harvard professor who a few years ago advocated bombing out all Vietnamese villages is representative of the American intellectual elite.

At the same time, when I spoke just now of the original dream of the early East European Zionists, I didn't mean to draw too rosy a picture of the present. We have our share of bigots and zealots. We are not at all another Eden or the kingdom of saints purged of all sin that the early Zionists had envisaged. We are a country like many others but we live under the dreadful stresses of an unending war and with the memory of the Holocaust still fresh in our minds. It is not what Herzl or Weizmann or Martin Buber or Magnes had visualized in their youth.

Israel is a good example illustrating that no revolution can ever be programed. And no wonder! What was planned as an orderly exodus became a desperate escape from the gas chambers of Europe. What was planned as a model society developed as a fortress state, threatened continuously by ferocious enemies. What was planned as a safe haven became entrapped in near-permanent war. The early Zionists were humanists, liberals, pacifists and social democrats with an instinctive abhorrence of all prejudice and all violence. They were proven wrong in the end. It was their fault, but not only theirs. In the 1930s their humanism made them reach out to the Arabs time and again in futile attempts to arrive at a compromise: by proposing a binational state or partition. The tragic truth is that they never found an Arab who was ready to speak to them. They ended by speaking mostly to themselves.

Hassan: But subsequently things changed in Israel, didn't they?

Elon: Yes, they did. The early innocence of the humanist Zionists survived decades of Arab intransigence. I suspect that innocence came to an end with the rise of Nazism and the collapse of civilization in Europe. The ideal of building a model society was overshadowed now by the exigencies of rescue: save as many Jews as you possibly can from the sinking ships of Europe. The Zionist leaders had only limited means at their disposal. In the late 1930s there was not yet an Israel state. The frustration of fighting Arab opposition and British immigration restrictions to Palestine left a deep imprint. A new nationalism emerged, less lofty, more self-centered.

It's important to remember that very few Jews, relatively speaking, were rescued through immigration to Palestine before 1939, and after 1939 the gates were shut. Between 1940 and 1945 the Jews of Europe were led like sheep to the slaughter. I wish I could make it really clear to you, Sana. I speak here of what are probably the two most important features of the Israeli national character: one is the trauma generated within Israel by the Nazi Holocaust; the other is an existentialist sense of self-assertion in adversity. Consider this background, and now place yourself in an Israeli's shoes. At the moment when some Arab leader is threatening us with extinction, whether as a people or even as a political entity, can you imagine the impact it has, the associations it immediately evokes, the fears it generates and our determination to resist?

Hassan: I understand how the Israelis feel, Amos, and I do sympathize. I am sure that if I were in your shoes, I would be full of those same fears and anxieties. But try also to understand the Arabs. They are not Nazis and there are no gas chambers waiting for you in Cairo even if we do win. To us, your tendency to project from past experience seems like paranoia. I personally know that it is not. But I do wish, although this is perhaps too much to ask of you, that despite the traumas you have experienced, you would try to break free from your fixation with the past.

Elon: Look, Sana, you can be a paranoic, utterly fixated on the past, and still have a lot of real and dangerous enemies. If many of us equate your enmity with anti-Semitic pogroms, this is a stereotype which is all too often reinforced by Arab propaganda. Some Arab publicists have hailed Adolf Eichmann as a "hero who fell in the Holy War."

In the past twenty years a vast literature of downright racism calling for genocide has been published in Egypt and Lebanon, often by government-owned publishing houses. You probably know that this racism has penetrated even school textbooks for Arab children. When the Israeli army entered the Gaza Strip in 1967, they found dozens of such textbooks issued by the Egyptian Ministry of Education. In tone and content, even in their graphic illustration, these textbooks resembled the worst Nazi propaganda during World War II. Or take, for example, the published records of an Egyptian government-sponsored conference of Islamic scholars from all over the Arab world. It took place in 1968 in Cairo and was formally welcomed by the Vice-President of Egypt.

Seventy Muslim priests discussed the theological significance of the Arab-Israeli war. I'm not citing Israeli propaganda to you now, Sana. They published a full transcript themselves in three fat volumes. It is a shocking document and it is the kind of thing that causes Israelis to associate you with the worst of the Nazis. The recurring themes of that conference, and I quote from the transcript, were: 1) Jews are the "enemies of God." 2) Jews are the "dogs of humanity," not only now but even in Biblical times. Their evil has been transmitted through history to this day and Israel is simply the culmination of these historically and culturally deprived people. 3) The superiority of Islam and Arabism will be demonstrated in a future military victory over the Jews in which they shall all perish.

The fact that these Muslim priests knew the moral depravity which similar slogans of hatred had generated in Nazi Germany did not inhibit them from repeating these ideas in the most virulent form. Nor did it stop the Egyptian government from sponsoring that conference.

And there's much more to it. The infamous *Protocols of the Elders of Zion** have been published and republished under the auspices of the Egyptian government in Cairo at the expense of your taxpayers. Not since the Nazis has that calumny been republished except in Cairo and in other Arab capitals. Nasser himself once recommended the book to an Indian visitor as an "important insight" into the Jewish character. He told that Indian visitor, and I quote from the official collection of President Nasser's speeches and press interviews, "It is important that you read these *Protocols of the Elders of Zion.* I will give you a copy. It proves beyond all doubt that three hundred Zionists, each knowing the others, control the fate of the entire European continent and elect their successors from among themselves." What would you say to this?

Hassan: I know it may be too much to ask of you, Amos, since you are only one generation removed from Ausch-

* The *Protocols* (concocted by a defrocked Russian priest early in this century) purport to be the transcript of an international conference of Jewish financiers, said to control the entire world and to plot the destruction of civilization.

witz, to look at this anti-Semitic filth with cold reason and detachment. I guess if I were in your place, I too would see a logical continuum between this anti-Semitic venom and the gas chambers. I think no matter what injustice the Israelis may have committed toward the Palestinians, it does not exonerate us from such acts. They are despicable and they will remain so, as blemishes on our record, to haunt us for generations to come. But I beg of you, Amos, for the sake of peace, make an effort to understand this.

Elon: I'd like to, Sana, but how can I understand it, except literally? Especially since it's accompanied so often by harrowing threats of physical and political annihilation.

Hassan: Well, try to understand that anti-Semitism is not rooted either in our history or in our religion or in our popular myths as it was in Europe. Arab history was relatively free from Jewish persecution before the twentieth century. Though there were some exceptions, they were rare. On the whole, our relationship with Jews was characterized by tolerance and protectiveness. Far from proclaiming the falseness of Judaism, our religion, unlike Christianity, actually confirms Judaism. Mohammed viewed himself as the last of a long chain of Jewish prophets. We say in our prayers, "May God bless our prophet, Abraham, and our prophet, Moses." There is no intrinsic conflict between our religion and yours, as there is between Christian doctrine, which maintains that the Saviour has come in the form of Jesus Christ, and Jewish doctrine, which denies this.

To be sure, when Mohammed was spurned by the Jews, he had some nasty things to say about them in the

Koran, but even then, his quarrel with them was over their behavior, not over your creed. The message he left us contains many positive references to the Jews. Today anti-Semitism is only a kind of war racism in the Arab world. It's the kind that Allied propaganda generated about the Germans in World War II, and the Americans about the Japanese, to mobilize popular emotion at home. It is intense and vicious, I don't deny that, but it's not endemic and it will burn out once the conflict is over. Arab governments did not exploit anti-Semitic sentiment, as in Germany. Rather, they had to manufacture it by importing anti-Semitic literature from abroad.

Elon: Even if it is not endemic, won't it leave a mark? You go on drumming racist hatred into the minds of schoolchildren and you will see the results somewhere. As long as you continue to believe in absurdities, you remain capable of committing atrocities. Even the racism of the Europeans is of quite recent origin. Religious persecution dates back to the Middle Ages, but the racism that fed the Nazis only started in Europe in the second half of the nineteenth century.

Hassan: Yes. If this conflict continues to fester, this racism could become endemic. This is all the more reason why we must end this conflict now. Even so, you must not project from the mere existence of anti-Semitic literature to the existence of anti-Semitic feelings. I do not doubt that such feelings exist among some marginal, mostly religious groups in the Arab world, but you cannot generalize from this to the vast majority of the Arabs. Years of being subjected to propaganda in the government-controlled press and on television and radio have made them relatively immune to all kinds of propaganda. They are bored stiff with propaganda whether it be about socialism or five-year plans, about Israel or against Jews. I tell you, the Arab people just don't believe it.

Elon: I very much hope you are correct. And yet, even if it is only "war racism," as you say, even if it is not endemic, it still goes on and on, and we, in Israel, go on hearing it all the time. Picture us, please, listening to this propaganda against the background of historical traumas, the morbid melancholy and the vast sadness which still permeate so much of Israel life. This combination explains a lot about us. It explains that prevailing sense of loneliness in the world which so many Israelis share, a sense of being utterly alone in a world which permitted the disaster to happen once, and may well permit it to happen again. It explains our obsessive suspicions, why we cling to everything we have. The average Israeli is convinced that the Jews of Europe were singled out to be massacred because they alone did not have the physical means to organize their defense. It explains our constant preoccupation with defense, our towering urge for self-reliance and for security: security in all possible forms, in borders, in psychological reassurance, in tangible—not implied—military arrangements. It explains why words and indirect promises are not enough, why we insist on borders more secure than those that have tempted aggression before. It explains also the rather Utopian notion of peace which the Israeli government has often had in the past. We yearn for a total peace, almost melodramatic reconciliation—Sadat and Golda falling into each other's arms. Everything short of that ideal peace is too risky, too dangerous. To be reliable, peace must be perfect.

Hassan: I understand your concern with security. It is legitimate, but I also believe that you should not make a fetish out of security and magnify your security needs beyond all realistic proportions. It paralyzes you and makes you forgo peace initiatives and thereby miss out on all opportunities for peace. It seems to me a real lack of imagination that in the years since 1967 you saw no alternative but to dig in, in Suez and Golan, and wait for us to agree to peace negotiations without any preconditions. Even if you found Sadat's peace soundings unconvincing, I am amazed that you never called his bluff. And I find it even more surprising, Amos, that you still talk to me about secure borders.

Elon: I speak of borders more secure than those we had before 1967, when Tel Aviv was within range of Arab artillery, a mere fifteen miles away.

Hassan: The Russians are now supplying a sophisticated missile system to the Arabs. These missiles could well reach Tel Aviv in another war, making your insistence on "secure borders" obsolete. It is this specter of mutual suicide that haunts me. I don't understand why you insist on the antiquated notion of "secure borders." You fared better in 1967, with far more precarious frontiers, than you did in 1973, with your so-called secure border. Geography is only one factor in guaranteeing security, along with many others such as the strength of political institutions, technology, economic resources, the alertness of your intelligence services, the quality of your armed forces and your international alliances—in the long run they are more important.

In any case, wouldn't demilitarized buffer zones patrolled by UN troops serve just as well to secure your borders? They would act as a trip wire which would give you ample warning in case of an Arab attack so that you could mobilize your troops. After all, the Bar Lev Line, which was manned by your own soldiers, along the Suez Canal, did not afford you any more protection than such troops would have done. Even Dayan has admitted that your reserve army is not large enough to sit eyeball to eyeball facing professional Arab armies to repel a massive first strike. Couldn't you make a mutual defense pact with the United States? Such a pact would deter any attack, just as the countries within NATO have been immune to attack because the degree of the American commitment to come to their defense is spelled out.

Elon: We have never been offered such a defense treaty by the United States. It would certainly change things if we were. On principle, I would prefer us all to get out from under the tutelage of the superpowers, but we don't live in a dream world, unfortunately. In the real world of domineering superpowers, Israel's security would undoubtedly increase if the United States guaranteed the invulnerability of our borders.

Conversely, your perennial fears of Israeli expansionism might be assuaged by a Soviet guarantee of your borders. The important thing is to mutually agree on your borders and on ours. There is, of course, a lot of truth in what you say about the insufficiency of borders. Real security grows from many factors, including where one nation ends and another begins. If the Arabs were less divided between militants and moderates, if there was more stability in the Arab countries, and if they would be more explicit in their desire to make real peace with us, the border issue would not loom so large. In that case, even Israeli "hawks" would not be so insistent.

Hassan: But if you were the Israeli Prime Minister, Amos, would you be prepared to broadcast to the Arab world a commitment to withdraw your troops from all areas except those absolutely essential for your security? Would you do so, excepting Jerusalem, where some accommodation will have to be made, but including all of the West Bank? That would encourage us and foster trust among us. And would you pledge to make a token withdrawal unilaterally, to initiate the mutual process of give-and-take for the sake of peace?

Elon: In 1967 I think I certainly would have committed us to token withdrawal to prove our good intent, and I also would have favored total withdrawal in return for a peace treaty. But now? After all that has happened since 1967? When there's still no offer of a U.S. defense treaty? When the Arabs are still so cagey about peace? My first emotional reaction now would frankly be this: "God, am I glad I'm not Prime Minister!"

I shudder at the thought that the decision to withdraw might endanger more lives and even the existence of

Israel as a state. One should be prepared to take risks for peace as one takes risks for war, but I would also like Israel to have borders slightly more secure than it had in 1967. It's an emotional gut reaction that I have, I admit.

Hassan: And I must admit that I am disappointed.

Elon: Well, what would you do if you were the President of Egypt?

Hassan: As President of Egypt I would not have turned a deaf ear to your peace soundings, as Nasser did in 1967. I would have responded eagerly to General Dayan's appeal that we telephone Tel Aviv. I would admit that our politics in the past were the result of misreadings of Israeli intentions, just as yours stemmed, to some extent, from a misreading of our intentions. Both sides had made mistakes. Our fault was that we refused direct negotiations with Israel and that we played up your worst fears through an extremist press and anti-Semitic literature. I would try to break through this distrust by inviting Israelis to come to Egypt, by sending Egyptians to Israel, by trying to get Israelis to write in our press and explain to us their point of view, by trying to write in your press and explain to you our point of view, by opening up telephone communications, mail, all kinds of communications, to allay your fears and build up your trust.

Elon: If you were President and said and did all that, I would gladly have made the announcement you just asked for. You would no more have any reason to be disappointed. I really wish you would run for the Egyptian presidency, and win it . . .

But seriously, I would like to add something here, Sana. From what I said before of Israel living under the impact of a traumatic past, you might get the impression of a people of three million neurotics, completely entrapped in obsessive fears to the exclusion of everything else. That would be misleading. While we are definitely a traumatized people, there has, at the same time, been a generational change. And the great influx of immigrants from the Arab countries, who did not experience Nazism personally or even indirectly through their relatives, is changing the temper and tone of the country.

If we are not the kingdom of saints that the early Zionists aspired to, a few important features have nevertheless survived of the faded dream. I mean, in Israel, by and large, the moral fiber of society has remained relatively intact. It makes life in Israel so worthwhile, despite the hardships and constant dangers. You can see this moral fiber in the attitude to human life, which remains sacrosanct despite the inevitable brutalization of living in constant war. You can see it in the fact that, thank God, we remain a free society.

Even this is surprising in a way. In a country that has lived through thirty years of military emergency, where the military consideration has, of necessity, been paramount over all other considerations, you would have expected long ago a government by tall, tough, crew-cut colonels—hard men, hardened by strife. Fortunately we are not governed by a military junta, but until recently by a bunch of septagenarians, and at times, wishy-washy civilians. People often speak of the Israeli miracle, making the desert bloom and so forth, but this is no miracle at all when you have the physical means. You did much the same thing in Egypt; and the Americans did it in Arizona. The true miracle of the Israeli enterprise is this moral fiber, the fact that we have remained an intensely civilian society, a fanatically civilian people. A lifetime of war has hardly enhanced the so-called martial virtues. We may be fighting our enemies like ferocious Spartans, but among ourselves we remain Athenians, as quarrelsome, as self-destructive in our contentiousness, as passionately argumentative—but also as free. There is a lot that is wrong, of course, with the political system, which the old East European establishment bequeathed to us. Many of us would like very much to change this system. The important thing is that we have remained free, and because of this, I think we'll be able to change it.

Hassan: Even your enemies would want to concede, perhaps grudgingly, that moral fiber of which you speak. I definitely think that it's to your credit. Your complacency, conceit and inertia sometimes drive me to despair of peace, but I draw new hope when I see that Israel still manages to produce army men like Meir Pail and Mati Peled (retired generals who spearheaded the move within Israel for moderation and territorial compromise), enlightened scholars like Shimon Shamir and Michael Bruno, writers like Amos Oz and yourself, journalists like Amos Kenan and Avnery, politicians like Eliav and Ben Aharon. These people hold Israel up to very rigorous standards of humanitarian behavior, as Weizmann and Buber did in their day.

When I look around me in the Arab world I envy you

these humane men of moderation, some of whom even come out of your army. I admire their courage to criticize and I admire the system that permits them to do this. I wish that we had more of both. Still, in the eyes of the Arabs, this moral fiber which is part of the heritage brought to Israel by its present East European rulers is counterbalanced by the rigidities stemming from their past experience. I don't think it would ever have been possible for Golda Meir to have freed herself from the impact of early childhood memories of pogroms.

That is why I am glad to see that a new generation, most of them native-born, is already replacing the old—men of moderation like Aharon Yariv, Yigal Allon, Haim Barlev and Yitzhak Rabin. They at least will not have those old hang-ups about us. They will look at us as normal human beings. They will not think of us either as barbarian Cossacks out for another pogrom or as primitive beings to whom they are bringing the benefits of their superior European civilization. The Israeli Deputy Prime Minister, Yigal Allon, not so long ago, said in a speech in the Knesset, supporting a more conciliatory policy toward the Arabs, that he did not know anything about Munich, he was born in the Galilee. I hope he meant that his political frame of reference is not Europe of 1938 but the Middle East of 1974. I sighed with relief when I heard this. How typical do you think that attitude is?

Elon: It is true that men like Allon and Rabin have fewer hang-ups than Golda Meir. But don't make too much of it. We have a long way to go. This is a real political con-

flict between two national movements, not a misunder-
standing as a result of someone's psychological hang-ups.
It will take a lot before even Rabin, and other Israeli
politicians of the younger generation, will be more trust-
ful of the Arabs. There must be some reciprocity. The
war must end, first. Then, on your side, the threats, the
rabble-rousing speeches and the terror must cease.

If we could at least point to a parallel to the present
process of generational change in Israeli politics with similar changes in the Arab countries, we would already
have achieved a lot. You're right, to a certain extent,
about the changed perception of the younger generation
in Israel. Their approach is existential, as the older generation was prompted by ideology. They take Israel for
granted, in a simple, straightforward way. They don't
feel they have to moralize about it or prove something.
Rabin is native-born; he does not feel impelled, as Golda
Meir did, to justify his personal and political biography.
He tends to be pragmatic where the old leaders appear
doctrinaire. For example, he would never say that he
does not know what is meant by a Palestinian nation. In
this he is quite typical of the younger Israeli-born or
Israeli-bred generation. Face to face with the Palestinian
Arabs, the old generation in Israel tended to avert their
eyes; some resorted to wishful thinking or made sterile
and unfair comparisons with the Cossacks. Younger
Israelis rarely share this point of view. Even Moshe Dayan
has reflected this change. Let me read you a speech he
made a few years ago:

"In my youth I traveled a good deal with my late father
through the valley of Esdraelon. We used to meet Arabs.

At that time, especially in the winter, Arabs wrapped their faces in a kaffiyeh until only their nose and eyes remained exposed. My father was not born in this country. He came from Russia when he was seventeen. He would say to me, 'Look, they have the eyes of murderers.' But these Arabs were not murderers. It only seemed to my father that in the eyes which peered through the kaffiyeh's folds he saw the same look that he remembered from his Russian *shtetl*. But this didn't make these Arabs into murderers; it was winter and they were just covering their faces from the cold."

I only wish President Sadat, or some other prominent Arab leader, would present a similar speech to make the distinction between his father's image of us and his own perception of the Jew and the modern Israeli today.

Hassan: I'm sure that could help a great deal and push things forward in the right direction, but we can already see the beginning, the first glance of a new perception of Israel, in the eyes of prominent Arabs. True, Sadat has not yet spoken up, nor has Arafat, the leader of the Palestinians. But take, for example, Ali Amin, the new editor in chief of the well-known newspaper *Al Akhbar,* and one of the most prominent men in the country. I have the text of a recent interview he gave *Newsweek* in which he said:

"The scars will heal very quickly. As it is, most of our fears of Israeli domination have vanished as the result of October 6th. The Arabs now have undreamed-of billions of dollars and a tremendous supply of manpower. Soon we will have a new pool of technical know-how that will make the Middle East a unique part of the world and if we are happy and free and unsuspicious, as I think we will be, we will want the whole world to partake of this new age. We will have everything we need to make our deserts bloom and turn our mud huts into decent houses. Ignorance breeds prejudice and the ignorance will rapidly vanish. The Middle East is where East and West are finally going to come together. Perhaps I am a dreamer but I also see a United States of the Middle East. Israel will not be included in such a grouping in the foreseeable future, but once the Palestinian state is set up, it will obviously have to live in peace with its neighboring Jewish state. After, there are many hopeful options. The time has come for all of us to develop a more generous vision of the future and to act boldly and decisively. The establishment of a country the Palestinians can call their own will mean finally that the Arab countries and Israel can bury their differences. If you see the emergence of a Palestinian state, and the timing has never been more propitious than right now, I think that you will see an era of freedom and love the likes of which the world has seldom known."

Elon: Such sentiments, Sana, will certainly be echoed by a lot of Israelis. But does Amin make these statements to the Egyptian public too or only in interviews with the foreign press? You see, Sana, Dayan was addressing a public audience in Tel Aviv and later published the text in a book.

Hassan: Amin has not yet written in this vein in *Al Akhbar,* but I know that's what he tells Egyptians too. I know he reflects Sadat's point of view and that is also the way prominent Egyptians close to President Sadat speak. This is their basic outlook toward Israel. You ought to see them for what they really are—Egypt's counterpart to the pragmatic, moderate, native-born Israelis who are now coming up in Israeli politics. In your opinion, will the moderates be able to maintain a prominent position in the Cabinet?

Elon: I don't know. The Israel Cabinet is a coalition of several political parties, but these moderates have now gained a majority, at least within the upper echelons of the Labor party, which has always been and still is the kingpin of Israeli politics. As you know, we still have the proportional election system which never gives a single party a clear majority and imposes government by coalition. The whole country is regarded as one constituency: you vote for ideological parties and not for individual candidates. As a consequence, all Israeli Cabinets since 1948 have been coalitions between the dominant Labor party and a half-dozen small splinter parties. The Labor party has always been the biggest party, with between thirty to thirty-six percent of the popular vote, but to stay in power, they have to rely on the small splinter parties.

Many of us would like to change this antiquated system. It is a remnant of the old days of pioneering, ideally suited to the early society of sixty thousand highly motivated, highly ideological pioneers. It leaves much to be desired in the industrial urban mass society of three million we have today. By giving exaggerated leverage to the small parties in the coalition, it distorts the popular will.

Take, for instance, the National Religious Front. This party hardly represents ten percent of the national vote. As a result of its exaggerated leverage, it not only prevents the much needed separation of state and synagogue in Israel but also opposes withdrawal from the West Bank of the Jordan because of the Jewish holy places and historical sites there. Even though the pragmatic moderates now have the upper hand within the ruling Labor party, it is still under pressure from the intransigent right.

Hassan: I'm very worried about the undue influence of the religious party.

Elon: So am I. I would like our new borders on the West Bank to answer real security needs, rather than conform to religious sentiment, however salient ancient historical precedence. I would like those new borders to be open, with Arabs and Israelis permitted to cross freely as visitors or residents. But I'm frankly scared by the explosive mixture of religion and chauvinism which is often at the root of the religious party's attitude. It presumes to make territorial claims in the twentieth century in the name of what God and Abraham are said to have told each other in the Bronze Age.

Apart from all that, we have a right-wing opposition party, the hard-line Likud, which is even more intransigent than the National Religious Front. The men of Likud have a similar tendency to quote the Bible selectively. In the Bible there is not only a Joshua but also an Isaiah. If the Israeli Labor party doesn't soon sort out its internal problems—the question of succession and generational change within its upper echelons—the Likud opposition may well increase its strength and in the next elections replace the Labor party as the kingpin of our next government coalition.

Hassan: We, too, unfortunately, have our hard-liners. They are waiting for an opportunity to pull the rug from under the moderates. What is happening within Egypt and the Arab world is in many ways a mirror image of what is happening in Israel. The hard-liners distrust the Americans. They feel that the most the United States is interested in is crisis management, diffusing hostility by granting the Arabs a few tidbits in return for their oil. They fear that in the long run the United States will leave them in the lurch because the Americans are not interested in a peace settlement which would oblige them to put pressure on Israel. They are also worried about Egypt putting all its faith in one man, Henry Kissinger, who, after all, is not an institution.

Then, there are still people among us who aspire to the total destruction of Israel. These people in Egypt have many allies among hard-liners in Libya, Iraq, among the Palestinians and most notably in Syria. Many Syrians are convinced that the United States is out to isolate the Arabs from their only reliable ally, the Soviet Union. They think that Sadat plays along with the United States because he puts his own immediate gain above the interests of the Syrians and the Palestinians. We Arabs suffer from another handicap. Because Israel is a free society, the public is aware of the limitations of the partial victory in 1973. It feels discouraged and tired of war.

Unfortunately, because Egypt is not a free society, only the very top leaders know that they were in a pinch in the '73 war, and because of that, they have no appetite for a renewal of the conflict. The public, on the other hand, really believes that we *won* that war, and sometimes even screams for a renewal of warfare. There is another danger: because Egypt is a closed society, when new leaders take over from the present ones, they may not have the information which tempered the policies of their predecessors. Even some of the present leaders, unfortunately, have a selective memory. They forget their narrow escape in 1973 and remember only the illusion of success.

Elon: It sounds like touch and go, Sana. Both in the Arab countries and in Israel. I ask myself if we are going to find the time or the strength to sort it all out internally before it is too late.

There's an old Hasidic tale of the great Rabbi Nachman of Bratzlav, who one day was traveling through a wintry mountain region in a carriage pulled by two oxen. When the carriage reached a steep hill, he got off and walked alongside in the mud to ease the animal's burden. The coachman reproached him and urged him to get on again. "I don't want to reach the pearly gates," said the old man, "and find these two oxen there complaining to the Creator that this fat old Jew remained in his seat while they were slaving under the yoke." "But they won't be able to argue that," said the coachman. "They are oxen; it is their job to pull the carriage up the hill." "Yes," said the rabbi, "that is true, but who has the strength to argue with oxen?"

We'll just have to have the strength, Sana, both in Israel and in the Arab countries.

Hassan: Over fifty percent of all Israelis are of Oriental origin. They either emigrated from Arab countries or were born of parents from Morocco, Algeria or Yemen. What influence do you think they will have on Israeli politics?

Elon: This is very hard to predict. They or their parents are new in the country—having arrived barely twenty-five years ago, at most—to leave a decisive mark on politics. But they are already quite prominent within local party machines, on municipal councils and on the back benches of the major parties.

Hassan: Most Arabs believe that if only the Oriental Jews were in power, we would get a much better deal. They keep saying that the Oriental Jews are really Arabs and that they would understand us better.

Elon: That's an illusion. To illustrate what you say, Sana, at one point, a few years ago, Radio Damascus was beaming special broadcasts of Iraqi or Syrian music into Israel in the hope of stimulating Iraqi patriotism among Israeli Jews of Iraqi origin . . . By the same reasoning, they broadcast German beer-hall music, introducing the program with the remark, "And now for our friends from Berlin . . ." They hoped to make people in Israel homesick for Germany so that they would go back there.

Hassan: That's a good example of how we fail to see one

another the way we really are. And it's not funny, it's tragic. I myself think the common Arab belief that Oriental Jews will understand us better is downright naïve. My personal experience has been that this is perhaps true only of some middle-class Jews from Egypt who never underwent the kind of persecution that was meted out to Jews in Iraq, Syria or Yemen. Such Egyptian Jews sometimes speak nostalgically of *la belle vie en Égypte,* but they represent only a small group among Israel's Oriental Jewry. I don't blame the rest for their bitter feelings. I suppose if I were in their place, and had undergone what they went through, I might feel the same way, but I think that they are just as much prisoners of their past traumas as the East Europeans are of theirs. Let's hope that a new unburdened generation will soon come up.

Elon: In the second generation the differences between Israelis of European and of Oriental origin are slowly evening out through education, economic improvement and a shared sense of collective experience. I won't belittle the tremendous difficulties remaining. But intermarriage between European and Oriental Jews is now about twenty percent, and it is rising at the rate of one percent annually. At this rate, the entire distinction between European and non-European Israelis may disappear in another thirty or fifty years.

3

Israel and Egypt

Hassan: The Arab governments, I think, are now prepared to talk peace with Israel.

Elon: Well, Israel was always prepared to talk. Israel was prepared to make compromises both in territory and in principle. Why did it take you so long to be ready to talk and to recognize the facts for what they are?

Hassan: Come on, Amos, aren't you being unfair and very simplistic here? I mean, the facts of which you talk are that both of us were at fault. I'm not denying, you know, our role in the difficulties, but certainly there was a lot of fault on your side too. First of all, for a long time most Israelis were afflicted with a kind of moral myopia: either they did not recognize the Palestinian presence or else they thought wishfully that if they just ignored the Palestinians, they would go away. It's only very recently that Israelis have had to contend with the fact that the problem wasn't simply going to go away and that some positive initiatives had to come from your side.

I think that there were times when you could have come forth with constructive actions; but you dragged your feet, you didn't do it. After 1967 you sacrificed peace for internal political considerations, mainly because you didn't want to talk about the controversial issue of territorial concessions. Such concessions might have split the Labor party that rules Israel. Your leaders preferred, therefore, to settle for a stalemate. So you're being unfair in casting sole blame upon us, because, certainly, since 1970, we have made many overtures to you which you just ignored.

Elon: Really? What overtures did you make after 1970?

Hassan: Well, for example, just the fact that in July 1970 Egypt accepted United States Secretary of State William Rogers' peace plan was a big concession. You don't realize to what extent President Sadat had to stick his neck out to do that. The peace plan, proposed by Mr. Rogers in 1969, in fact implied recognition of the state of Israel, since it demanded that in exchange for a return of conquered territories, the Arabs sign a peace treaty with Israel. Certainly this would have granted de jure recognition to Israel.

Elon: Secretary Rogers spoke generally of "establishing peace"; he did not specify "signing" a peace treaty. Israel wanted you to *sign* a peace treaty as a test of your intentions. An implied peace, through papers deposited with a third party, the United States or the United Nations, was not enough.

And you are wrong if you think that "internal considerations" prompted Israel to reject the territorial concessions implied in the Rogers peace plan. The real reason was fear. We were too afraid of you. Our fears were justified by the bitter experience of the past. This is why we insisted after 1970 on new borders, not for aggrandizement but for protection; we asked for better borders, more defendable than the old, which had tempted aggression too often; we wanted and still want *new* borders, not dictated, but *mutually* agreed upon by the sides.

After all, this conflict didn't start in 1970; it started fifty years before and these fifty years had been filled with Arab threats to throw us into the sea. We never threatened *you* with genocide. I suppose that we still are very much afraid of you; and you still give us lots of good reasons.

Hassan: I am tempted to answer you by saying that while we threatened to throw you into the sea, you actually threw us into the desert. But that would be only nice rhetoric. It is unfair of you to keep using the demagogic statement of an extremist Palestinian leader as if it were representative of the entire body of our political thinking. It's as if I cited to you as representative of your government's position the statement of an extremist in Israel who says that "Israel extends from the Nile to the Euphrates."

Elon: Sana, excuse me, but this is nonsense. No Israeli extremist—not even the most intransigent—ever claimed that Israel should extend from the Nile to the Euphrates. How long will you believe in this myth?

Hassan: I will grant you that there are only a few such people and that unlike in the Arab countries, they are outside the political power spectrum. I mentioned it only as an example of unrepresentative rhetoric. But seriously, Amos, couldn't we move beyond the past! If you continue to attribute the worst possible motivations to us, then, inevitably, you make a lot of policy decisions based on sheer force and you block all the *political* options available to us. This is what you did in the past, when we finally went to war in October 1973. Because you left us no option, the war became a self-fulfilling prophecy.

The way we see it, the 1973 war was forced upon us by your rigidity, by your policy based on force, and by your takeover of our lands. If you had only taken the trouble to listen; we made many peace soundings last year which you were deaf to. Last year, and in 1972, Sadat was really desperate for peace. Kissinger himself told a group of American Jewish intellectuals—the interview was reproduced in an Israeli newspaper—that at least some of the Arab states would have been glad last year to settle for demilitarized zones, and to recognize Israel in return for their occupied territories. Kissinger reportedly blames himself for not having encouraged you to respond to that.

Elon: Well, the trouble was that if indeed Sadat wanted peace, he did little to make this clear to us. And even if you say he did, can you really isolate the events that took place after 1971 from what happened before? The 1973 war was not the first war; the conflict is at least half a century old.

But I agree, Sana. We should let bygones be bygones and agree that both sides are at fault. If so, don't we then have the first basis on which a reasonable discussion can be held?

Hassan: Definitely. Let's all be less self-righteous.

Elon: This by itself could be a momentous break. In the past, at least for the Arabs, there was little possibility of a compromise. And we Israelis were probably too arrogant, even when we proposed terms. But at least we never denied your rights as absolutely as you denied ours. Yet in the Arab mind, the Arab-Israeli conflict was always a clash between absolute right and absolute wrong, excluding all possibility of meeting us halfway. You talked yourself into believing that it was "morally impossible."

Hassan: That's true. Unfortunately, the Arabs tended to see things in black-and-white only. If you weren't angels, then you must be devils. I believe this was a hangover from the latter part of Arab history when the Arab empire went into decline and Islamic thinking became frozen in dogma and very authoritarian. The Arabs did not have the advantages of the European cultural Renaissance and of the relativistic and more pragmatic modes of thinking. This is why they seem unable to understand that they could be right and that the Israelis could be right too. But they are changing, and that's the important thing.

Elon: But they still don't grant that we have a moral case too. They are simply saying they can't liquidate us *now*.

Hassan: I will grant you that the change is not due to any greater understanding on our part of the moral legitimacy of your claim to Israel, or to any sudden change of heart. Rather, it is due to the failure to regain from Israel the territories conquered in the 1967 war, either by diplomatic or by military means. Nasser had at first hoped that he would be able to regain these territories by offering you some minor concessions, like the rights of navigation in the Gulf of Aqaba and the Suez Canal. He believed that you would settle for something short of peace and that by clever diplomacy he could drive a wedge between the United States and Israel, with the result that the United States would pressure you into accepting these terms.

When these tactics failed, Nasser turned from diplomacy to military action, by beginning what came to be called the War of Attrition. He counted on exhausting you by relentless shelling on the Suez front; he knew that with your small population, you would be less able to sustain the heavy casualties that this kind of static warfare inflicts.

As you know, in the years 1969–1970 Israel was badly hurt by this war. However, even the War of Attrition did not achieve Nasser's goals. He was unable to involve the Soviets in an all-out war against you. The most the Soviets were prepared to do was to commit their military advisers and pilots to the Suez front. It was at this point, then, that Nasser realized that having failed in both his military and diplomatic endeavors to get you to settle for concession short of peace, he had to make peace. Unfortunately, however, by 1970—by the time we had come around to readiness for negotiation—you guys had considerably hardened your position.

Elon: Really now, Sana, what makes you say we "hardened our position"? You just drew a very curious picture of the late President Nasser. All he wanted really was to get his territories back! What you don't mention is that he didn't lose them to a natural disaster but as a result of his own aggressive ambition. He lost the territories, and he lost almost his entire army, because he cynically precipitated the war of 1967—to the horror of the entire world. And after that war his cynicism, his utter callousness, came to a head once more in the moves you, Sana, have just described.

Hassan: I do not want to defend Nasser, or his policies, many of which I don't agree with. But I think that the demonic image which you and so many Israelis have of Nasser is somewhat childish and naïve. Your interpretation of Nasser's motivations is oversimplistic. It is true that he exploited the Arab-Israeli conflict for his own personal ambition and self-aggrandizement, but it is also true that he was a patriot, subject to the traumas which have shaped the nationalist aspirations of so many Arabs: a deep sense of humiliation due to centuries of weakness vis-à-vis European imperialists—humiliation reinforced by Israeli mistreatment of the Palestinians which the Arabs felt unable to rectify in the face of your superior military power, technological know-how and organizational skills.

When Nasser as a young officer suffered defeat at your hands in the 1948 war, he underwent once more the sense of frustration and impotence that Egypt had inherited, after a long period of colonial vassalage, an inept army and a corrupt decadent government. He was never really fighting you, he saw himself as fighting another imperialist overlord.

Elon: But we were never his overlords, neither in 1948 nor in 1967, nor in 1969, when he launched his War of Attrition, as you said, to wear us out by inflicting casualties on us. It is well known that Israel takes casualties very badly. The sacredness of human life is deeply ingrained in the Israeli, in the Jewish temper. What utter cynicism Nasser displayed! At least ten times as many Egyptians as Israelis were killed in the War of Attrition. Nasser must have felt that Egyptian human lives are expendable— ready cannon fodder for the realization of a political aim. Moreover, he was also prepared to let the entire Suez Canal Zone go up in flames and the cities of Suez and Ismailia, Qantara and Port Said reduced to rubble, and to watch hundreds and thousands of Egyptians, the inhabitants of these cities, go homeless. What cynicism!

Hassan: You exaggerate in your depiction of his cynicism. Nasser, as an Arab leader, nurtured a very genuine grievance against you, one which you did little to assuage. The most you can accuse him of is of being a reckless gambler, of taking too many risks to redress that grievance. You cannot accuse him of malicious intent in the

'67 war, or in the War of Attrition. He stumbled into the '67 war as a result of his bluff being called. He miscalculated when he first asked for UN troops to be removed from the Sharm el Sheik area; he did not expect that the UN would oblige so readily.

In the War of Attrition in 1969 he did not plan to have all those refugees on his hands. You are ignoring the time sequence. At first, in retaliation for Egyptian shelling, the Israelis bombed only selective targets in the Canal Zone with little damage to civilian centers. Nasser did not realize the risks to his own people.

Elon: But what poor judgment he showed, as a leader, how irresponsible he was, to imagine that he could control the nature and extent of our response to Egyptian provocation.

Hassan: It was a serious miscalculation, but it was only later that Nasser realized that he was unable to contain the war and would have to evacuate women and children from Suez. And only when, still later, the Israelis launched their massive bombing, did he realize the extent of the disaster that he had brought on himself. But he could hardly have foreseen that kind of massive retaliation on your part. Dayan himself was later to admit that Israeli military overreaction was a strategic error because it brought in the Russians, who set up missile installations to rescue Nasser and to protect the Egyptian cities from further Israeli bombings.

As to your statement that human life is not valuable for us, Israelis are forever saying how much more you care about your casualties because Israel is a very small country and everyone is so aware of losses. I think that this kind of statement has a racist bias.

You are completely oblivious to the emotions of our side. You dehumanize us. You don't see real Arabs, you see Arabs fabricated by the media, ferocious lynch mobs with murderous eyes, screaming for your blood. Such fanatic mobs get attention on television, but sorrowing Arab faces do not.

We were haunted by our casualties. How could we not have felt so when your bombing created over a million refugees? Cairo, a city already choking on its population of six million, had to absorb the bulk of these additional people made homeless by Israeli military action. We saw them everywhere, sleeping in the streets and in the grave-yards of the City of the Dead. They were crouching on hospital floors. I will never forget the stench and the moans of those wards.

Elon: If Nasser had not started the War of Attrition, there would have been no need to evacuate the civilians. They could have remained living in their cities. There is a continuous inconsistency in your reasoning. You sharply criticize Nasser for his adventurism—more sharply than any other Arab so far—but you make us responsible for the consequences. He deliberately exposed the civilian populations of Ismailia and Suez to inevitable havoc caused by his war. These cities were right on the Suez Canal front line. He was like a robber holding up a bank surrounded by his own children as hostages, expecting the guards not to shoot at him to save their lives.

President Sadat is now rebuilding the cities of Suez

and Ismailia. Egypt could have saved itself the expense and the agony by not starting the War of Attrition in the first place. Nobody would have been hurt if Egypt had been ready for peace talks instead, or if Nasser had had as much concern and thought for his own casualties as we have for ours.

Hassan: Of course we care for our casualties as much as you care for yours. I can only quote to you a letter, from his wife, to an Egyptian soldier who was killed by the Israelis in the 1967 war. I must say, to your credit, that this letter was published in Israel and in the Israeli best seller about the war called *The Seventh Day*. I would like to quote to you the full text of what she wrote her husband a few days before he was killed:

"I long for your dear presence as a sick man longs for health, as a student craves success, as the plants long for water, as a baby desires its mother's tender embrace.

"If one could send greetings on the waves of the sea, I would send a greeting on every wave, thousands and thousands of greetings—and if I could send you peace with doves, I would send you millions of greetings with every feather of their plumage. My husband and my eternally beloved, beloved of my heart, when will I see you, my darling, light of my eyes and breath of my soul?

"May God preserve you, my darling husband, faithful and true. Greetings to you. Please answer quickly and let me know how you are so that our minds may be set at rest here. And may peace come soon.

"Saida Ahmed Salah"

Elon: Who could deny that the common people of all

nations at war suffer, that soldiers bleed and their wives weep? That is not what I question. The Nassers make mistakes, the Ahmed Salahs pay the price. It was Nasser's cynicism that horrified me, his willingness to precipitate a bloody war not only for his own people, but for the entire world.

When Nasser realized he was not breaking us in the War of Attrition, he desperately tried to get the Soviet Union to enter the war as a belligerent on Egypt's side. Here he was even risking the possibility of a world war and a nuclear holocaust, for surely the United States could not have stood idly by while the Soviets were making war in the Middle East.

Here is the bitter irony: during this entire time Nasser could have gotten all, or almost all, of the lost territories back if he had only been ready to utter the word "peace." He said so himself. In 1968 Nasser publicly admitted that he could get the entire Sinai back if he only went to Tel Aviv to shake hands with the Israeli Prime Minister—at the time, Mr. Levi Eshkol—and sign a peace treaty. He said himself that he didn't want to do it.

Everybody knows that in the aftermath of the 1967 war, Israel was ready to relinquish the bulk of the occupied territories that were conquered from Egypt in the war which Nasser cynically precipitated in 1967. Nasser refused. He remained loyal to the decision he and the other Arab rulers had adopted in August 1967, only two months after the war. At their conference in Khartoum they decided solemnly that there must be no recognition of Israel, no negotiations with Israel, no peace with Israel. This decision, Sana, was a disaster—don't you agree?

Hassan: I agree. Khartoum was an unmitigated disaster. I thought so at the time and still think so now. But even so, you must not persist in seeing Nasser as a devious, Machiavellian figure who had a complex plan for destroying the world. Nasser never believed that trying to draw the Soviets into the war on our side would lead to a nuclear confrontation; he never expected the Americans to go to war for Israel's sake because the American population was so sick and tired of the Vietnam war. It is true that Nasser did miss many opportunities for peace after '67, but you have to realize that making peace with you after '67 would have been tantamount to submitting to the humiliations of a dictate. Because of this, it was very, very difficult. Peace could hardly spring from such a sense of humiliation.

Elon: Sana, your analysis of Nasser, with all your qualifications and explanations, ex post facto, is an even more crushing condemnation of the man than mine. What a series of disastrous errors and miscalculations did you just describe—all paid for by innocent young lives on both sides. I say, God save us all from such leaders, who stumble from one disaster to another. It is the stuff of all the horror stories in human history. How fortunate we are that the Soviet Union had a better understanding and a greater sense of statesmanship and a better awareness of American intentions than Nasser had, and refused to stumble into an even greater disaster by joining the war on Nasser's side. They knew well that such action might lead to a nuclear war.

And the bitter irony is that Nasser could have avoided

the senseless bloodshed on your side and on ours. He could have prevented the destruction of your cities. Hundreds of thousands of Egyptians would still be living in their homes in Suez and Ismailia. Egypt would have gotten all its territories back—if only Nasser had been ready to make peace! You call that submitting to the humiliations of a dictate? What do you mean? He starts a war, in the course of which he loses territory. He is offered this territory back in return for a signed peace. You call this a dictate, Sana? I call it a generous settlement for a man who probably did not deserve it.

Hassan: I myself did not feel that making peace at that time would have been a dictate. But the Arabs did suffer one of the most humiliating defeats in their history. It took you a mere six days to reduce their armies to rubble. In view of that, is it not reasonable of you to allow them a little time to make the psychological adjustment necessary to come to terms with you, to make peace with you and to accept the legitimacy of your state? They believed that if they came to the bargaining table completely in the nude, with their armies completely crushed, you would take advantage of their weakness. While you had indicated some willingness to return territory to Egypt, you had not said anything about the other Arab counrties.

Elon: That is true. I am very sorry we didn't. We should have expressed the same willingness to the other Arab countries as well.

Hassan: As the Arab leader who had led them all into this war, Nasser could not simply settle with you on his own and tell the other Arab countries to go hang themselves.

You expressed your outrage earlier about the speech Nasser made in 1968 in which he admitted that if he went and shook hands with Levi Eshkol, he could get Egyptian territory back. But don't you see that as a responsible Arab statesman, he had to take this position? In Arab eyes this speech was admirable because it indicated that Nasser was not prepared to sell them out. In the speech you are quoting, Nasser was in fact telling his soldiers, whom he was visiting on the front while they were preparing for the War of Attrition against Israel, "Don't think that you are preparing for this war just to get Egyptian territory back. If all we wanted was Egyptian territory, I could achieve that by shaking hands with Levi Eshkol. You are preparing for and you must sacrifice for the liberation of *all* Arab land, not only that of Egypt."

Elon: I agree that Nasser was entrapped, dazzled by his Pan-Arabic ambition, drunk and obsessed with his power as the unchallenged leader of Egypt, the glamor boy of all Arab nationalists everywhere in the Middle East. He felt he had to go on fighting that senseless war, casualties notwithstanding.

You asked why we did not give him time to adjust psychologically to the need to come to terms with us. Didn't we? Let me give you a rough idea of the feelings that *we* had at the time you speak of. Try to see it from this aspect too. In Israel during the first months after the 1967 war, we all felt sure that this had been the last war, that now surely there would be peace. In retrospect it seems naïve, but at the time we lived in a state of euphoria—not for having scored a victory, not for having escaped destruction, but over the possibility of peace after so many years of war.

But this was not to be. And the effect on us of that realization was traumatic. Instead of peace, Nasser started a massive rearmament program. Fifteen thousand Soviet technicians and military advisers arrived in Cairo. Instead of peace, the crazy speeches in Cairo continued. Instead of making peace, Nasser launched the War of Attrition. We suffered casualties, but we decided to hold on.

The Israeli press habitually prints the picture of each fallen soldier on the front pages of the newspapers. Imagine, Sana, opening the papers and finding almost daily the faces of dead nineteen-year-olds staring at you. Israel is not really a state, it's almost a clan in its intimacy, no death is ever anonymous but is a shared blow.

Why was Nasser doing that? It seemed to me at the time that we were facing a lunatic foe, a surrealist hostility, inexplicable, primitive, barbarian, beyond all reason. The situation imbued us with a loneliness and a grim determination to hold on, to bear the casualties even as we mourned them. We would not let Nasser wear us out. There seemed almost no hope in waiting for reason to prevail, someday, somewhere, in Egypt.

Hassan: Amos, of course this senseless suffering, these terrible deaths are extremely painful to me. War is horrible and frightening on both sides of this conflict. I can remember my own fears, even as far back as the 1956 war when I was only a child. The building in which we lived used to tremble when you bombed military bases on the outskirts of Cairo. Sirens would screech in the middle of the night and I would frantically scramble down the stairs with my parents. I can remember the look of terror in my mother's eyes as we huddled close together in the garage.

Each time there was a war, we were sure that you would bomb Cairo. In 1967 I worried terribly about my father, who was then an old man. I was afraid he might die of a heart attack or nervous exhaustion in one of those anguished races to the fallout shelters. Last October I begged my parents, who were in Europe, not to return to Egypt until it was clear that the cease-fire would hold.

Surely, we must learn to use this tragedy for both sides as an incentive to us to find peace, not as a paralyzing impediment.

Elon: It was not we who stood in the way of peace. In 1970, finally, the United States successfully sponsored a cease-fire along the Suez Canal that put an end to the War of Attrition between us. But the ink had hardly dried on the cease-fire agreement than Nasser broke it and moved the new Soviet missiles up the Canal in violation of the agreement. Consider, Sana, the impact of all this on the average Israeli. It generated new fears on top of old ones, as if there had not been enough of those already. If in the immediate aftermath of 1967 Israel was ready to give back all the territories seized from Egypt, as a consequence of later events, there grew a feeling among us that we could no longer afford to withdraw from all areas occupied in 1967. We had to keep you at a distance; we needed better borders than those that had tempted aggressors in the past, borders easier to defend, with great stretches of demilitarized zones between us and you to prevent another war of attrition.

Hassan: My God! What a tragedy for all of us. Just at this point the Egyptian position, for the first time, was beginning to change. Just then, in the fall of 1970, Nasser died and a new President took over. Anwar Sadat really wanted peace, but unfortunately, you didn't catch on because of your fears.

Elon: You say, Sana, that Sadat wanted peace? Perhaps one can look back and see that now. At the time, his message never reached us.

Hassan: What do you mean, it never reached you? He made all those peace soundings, and you have the chutzpa to say that the message never reached you? In addition to agreeing to the Rogers peace settlement which would have granted you de jure recognition, in 1970, he wrote Gunnar Jarring, the UN Secretary General's special representative for the Middle East, that he would be willing to make peace with Israel. You reacted by saying, "How nice, what else?"

Sadat also agreed to the formulation proposed by President Nixon to our envoy, Hafez Ismail, last year, which spoke of reconciling Israeli security concerns with Egyptian sovereignty in Sinai.

As to your talk about security, there is no doubt that some of your security concerns are legitimate, but you also worked the shibboleth of security. You used the excuse of security to justify what became, in fact, a form of creeping annexation.

I don't doubt that part of the reason for not returning to us the territory you captured was a very deeply engrained fear of us and a deeply engrained distrust. But you surely will not deny there were other reasons as well: as time passed, you just got accustomed to having all this territory. It was very nice to have all this land, the oil wells of Sinai, a supply of cheap Palestinian laborers on the West Bank and those very nice markets which had opened up for you in the occupied areas.

I think I also can understand your insecurity in matters relating to military achievement. Perhaps you overreact both to success and to failure; you always have to reassure yourselves that you are not going to be slaughtered like sheep once again. This makes you arrogant in victory, whereas another people, with a different history, might have achieved a more balanced sense of self-confidence. Your arrogance may be a compensation for your inherent anxiety. It also, perhaps, makes you so dejected and so full of self-flagellation when you suffer a minor setback, as in the 1973 October war. Your past had made you deaf to our peace soundings. After 1970 you were so cocksure, you thought that you could stay put on our land, you didn't need to listen carefully to what we were saying.

Elon: Arrogant, Sana? I wish I could make you understand. It was not arrogance but fear, a fear justified by recent Egyptian attitudes and threats—even under President Sadat. I'm not at all convinced by your philosophizing on the Jewish character. The real chutzpa is in your attitude now. We did not overreact. We responded as most people would to very real threats. I shudder at the thought of how you would have reacted if we had threatened "to throw you into the sea." Or if Israel were an international center for racist anti-Arab propaganda just as Cairo is a center of racist anti-Semitic literature to this very day.

You cannot really pretend, Sana, that everything changed between us when Nasser died in 1970. If we had reason to fear Egypt up to the moment of Nasser's death, as you admitted, was there really no reason to fear Egypt a week later, simply because a new man had come into power?

The Soviets were still in Egypt. Egypt was still amassing arms and was preparing for another war like a ferocious giant. Even if one granted now, years later, that Egypt, under Sadat, was changing in a direction of peace, how tragic then that he did so little to convince us of his intentions. I mean directly, explicitly, publicly to us, not in veiled messages, or hidden in convoluted diplomatic notes to third parties, or in interviews to some Danish newspaper. For God's sake, why didn't he say, "I want to sign a peace treaty with Israel. I'm ready to live with Israel within mutually agreed borders"?

Hassan: Amos, you drive me to despair. I'm beginning to feel as if we were locked in a dialogue of the deaf and the dumb. What more do you want from Sadat? That he fall on his knees and beg your pardon for our past iniquities? I talk to you about formal messages, formal correspondence sent to Rogers and Nixon, and you talk to me about convoluted messages. I talk to you about statements made to periodicals like *Newsweek, Time* magazine, the *New York Times,* and you speak to me about obscure Danish newspapers. Sometimes I really feel that what we Arabs and Jews expect from one another is some kind of reconciliation, as in a melodramatic Russian novel where everybody falls weeping into each other's arms and begs for each other's forgiveness. Unfortunately there is not going to be any such romantic reconciliation between the extremes of our hatred for one another. Instead there is going to be a long, very painful and arduous time of peaceful coexistence. You cannot hang on to the territories and wait until the Arabs are ready to hand over peace in exchange, as though peace were a finished product. Peace is a process which we both have to work for together. It is never achieved once and for all. Like democracy, one has to constantly struggle to preserve it.

It is like the story told by the wonderful Israeli novelist Amos Oz, who said: "When I see two people fighting in the streets of Tel Aviv, which happens every day, the first thing I try to do is to separate them, to end the fighting" —not to force them to shake each other's hand and beg each other's pardon.

Elon: I would gladly settle for peaceful coexistence. I realize that genuine peace will come only after a long period of mutual adjustment. But you cannot side-step this need by obtuse references to a "process." And I don't expect the Arab who attacked me to fall into my arms or even shake my hand. I just expect him to stop shooting. And after so many hair-raising Arab threats in the past, a little

Arab demonstration of positive intentions might do a lot of good.

Hassan: Why do you constantly refer back to these threats? I understand your fears, but I wish that you would stop selecting evidence from the past. You are so fixated on past reality. There is always a lag in your perception.

You weren't expected to give up your fears the day after Nasser's death; but, in truth, you had three years in which these fears could have abated. You talk about the Soviet presence reinforcing these fears, but the Soviets have been out of Egypt since 1972. We expelled them, and yet, what effect did this have on you? Instead of making you more flexible, more conciliatory, it made you more intransigent than ever. You calculated that now you had nothing to fear. The Arabs could obviously not contend with your military superiority without the Soviets. And even the Americans were not likely to pressure you so hard to make concessions when they no longer feared an escalation of the conflict and a possible confrontation with the Soviets.

Elon: On the contrary, the expulsion of the Soviets from Egypt confirmed the view of many of us that we were facing an irrational opponent, unpredictable, whose faint suggestions of peace were unreliable. I felt at the time that if you wanted peace, you should have kept those Soviets in Egypt as a leverage in the negotiations, and if you wanted war, you should also have kept them on. I did not know what to make of the Soviets' expulsion from Egypt.

Hassan: I wish I could convince you. I was in Egypt all of last year. The temper of the whole country indicated a desperate wish for peace. Most of the Cabinet ministers I interviewed believed that Egypt was incapable of launching any kind of war against you. Therefore, they put all of their hopes in diplomatic moves, particularly in persuading the United States to pressure Israel to be more flexible. It was a small minority who believed that your greed and your inflexibility were such, that nothing short of another war would convince you to give up the territories.

Elon: Nothing of that attitude was evident to us. I've been waiting for years to hear an authoritative Egyptian voice assuring me that, as you say, Sadat is desperate for peace. If he was so desperate for peace last year, why on earth didn't he ever take up the long-standing offer by the Israeli government to sit down at the negotiating table and discuss the future peace settlement without any pre-conditions, without victors and vanquished?

Hassan: How could he discuss without any preconditions when you were giving every indication that a great deal of territory wasn't going to be returned? You forget that in recent years your policy hardened considerably. The Israeli government came forward with the Galili Plan, which talked of offering up land for sale to Israeli citizens on the occupied West Bank. You were setting up dozens of new settlements there and drawing up plans for a new town, Yamitt, to be built in Sinai.

At the same time you were asking *us* to come around without any preconditions. Can't you see that it was a vicious circle? It was your policy of creeping annexation which in turn justified the Arab demand that before they came to a negotiating table, you should promise to give up the land. You should have declared that in exchange for peace you would retain only those territories with strictly strategic value such as Golan, Sharm El Sheikh and some military settlements along the Jordan. This would have made it clear to us that the issue was security, not territory. Although we might not have agreed to some of these terms, bargaining could have ensued and some accommodation could have been reached regarding Jerusalem.

Elon: If you had come to the peace table, as we asked you, the negotiations could still have been without any preconditions. All these new settlements were wide open to negotiation, and we might well have given them up in return for a genuine peace. What a pity, then, that Sadat, desperate for peace, as you say, chose to demonstrate this by launching a surprise attack on October 6, 1973. How can you expect the Israelis to believe that only six to eight weeks before, Sadat's most ardent desire had been a peaceful solution?

Hassan: Well, you drove him into a corner by trying to rub his face in the dust, by leaving him absolutely no alternatives, so that anything short of a devastating Egyptian defeat would be viewed by him as a victory. You thought that Sadat would never launch a war because he would be sure to lose it, but Sadat saw even a partial Israeli setback as a victory because it would break the stalemate.

Just look at what was happening in Egypt last year.

The situation was utterly untenable. Sadat was a laughingstock. The students were rioting. The soldiers were restless because they had been stuck in the trenches for five years to no purpose. The journalists were extremely critical and dissatisfied and they were being kicked out of their jobs en masse. Under those circumstances there was no way Sadat could hope to continue in power short of launching this war.

Elon: But couldn't Sadat, instead, have gone to Geneva for a peace conference with Israel, as he was prepared to do after the 1973 war? Wouldn't that have broken the stalemate, without still another terrible war?

Hassan: Well, he would have gone to Geneva if you had been willing to go then in the same spirit as you apparently are now. After 1970, all the moderates in Israel were silenced. The hard-line arguments had won over. Unfortunately it took this last war to soften you up. It's sad and ironic, but just as it took several hard knocks to make the Arabs come around to the inevitability of making peace with Israel, so for the Israelis, too, it took a bloody war, in which they lost over two thousand lives, to bring back a resurgence of the plea for moderation, for flexibility, vis-à-vis the Arabs.

Elon: Sana, aren't you being unfair to us? Israel had been crying out for a Geneva conference long before the 1973 war. That war did not get the Israelis to the peace table, it got the Arabs to the peace table when they saw, with their own eyes, that the war had ended in a stalemate. To continue fighting could have led to mutual suicide. That's when the Arabs, finally, after twenty-five years of war between us, decided to meet us at the peace conference.

Hassan: Is this really true, Amos? I believe we would have been happy to go to the peace table ever since 1970. We were waiting for the kind of invitation from you that would allow us to do so. Instead, you relied exclusively on force, exclusively on the creation of territorial *faits accomplis.* Many of the moderates in Israel who in 1967 would have been happy to exchange land for peace came to feel by 1970 that peace was too risky an enterprise. They decided that they could best rely upon military power as a deterrent. It was so good to hold on to the land that they felt it was not worth the trouble of shaking up the political status quo within Israel for a peace that they saw, at best, as precarious.

Elon: You gave us plenty of reasons. Our offer to meet at the peace table was repeated endlessly. You refused to meet. Instead, Sadat made grandiloquent pronounce-ments that 1972 would be the "year of decision." When that year passed, because he was still not sure that his army would win, he extended "the year" to 1973.

Hassan: But Sadat's "year of decision" did not necessarily mean war, Amos. It meant war *or* peace. What Sadat meant when he announced that 1972 would be the "year of decision" was that if you left him no way out, if you denied him the opportunity for a peace settlement, then he would be forced to go to war to regain the conquered territories—he was that desperate. It was your blunders and American blunders which ruled out the decision in favor of peace.

Two things, in my opinion, brought this about. First, we cheated on the cease-fire and moved the Soviet missiles closer to the Suez front, in July of 1970. This gave a tactical advantage to the Soviet Union. As a result, the United States felt that the only way the Soviets could be held in check was by a strong show of military support for Israel. Nixon responded with his first massive shipment of arms to Israel. It was a dramatic illustration of the commonality of U.S.-Israeli interests and demonstrated the usefulness of Israel as an ally to hold back the Soviets in the Middle East.

But second, and even more important, there was the Palestinian revolt against King Hussein in 1970. The fall of Hussein, as you know, would have meant a very drastic blow for U.S. interests in the area; a radical regime on the border of Saudi Arabia might have entailed the subversion of the Saudi Arabian regime itself. Israel thus became a very convenient ally. The Israeli threat to Syria prevented a more massive Syrian involvement on the side of the Palestinians. There were even coordinated plans for U.S.-Israeli intervention in favor of Hussein should Hussein's throne appear to be badly threatened.

I think that this was a crucial point in the history of Israeli-American relations. From then on the United States let the Israelis play the role of gendarme in the area. It became more and more amenable to persuasion by the Israelis to leave things alone, not to press them to make concessions, to let them handle the Arabs their own way—in other words, to settle for a stalemate and keep the Arabs at bay by sheer force.

Lastly, once the Soviets were out of the area, the United States decided that it no longer had to court Arab favor by pressuring you to return territories. Without the Soviet pressure, the United States could simply sit on her hands and hug the whole pie. And so it dropped its peace initiatives.

Elon: I'm afraid you exaggerate the extent of American influence on Israel. That influence certainly exists and it corresponds with U.S. global interests. But if you speak of the superpower's influence on us, isn't it even more true about you? Aren't you Arabs at least as much the instruments, the pawns, of the Soviets as we are dependent on the United States? And aren't the Soviets the real villains in this brutal game of power? Why, if Israel didn't exist, the Russians would have had to invent us! They penetrated the Middle East by exploiting your preoccupation with us. And how rich their rewards are!

For example, the Russians benefited directly from your use of the so-called oil weapon, which almost broke up NATO last fall. Compare the role of the United States and the role of the USSR in the Near East in the past decade. I certainly don't want to rhapsodize on American foreign and security policy, but on balance it seems clear that the United States always wanted peace in the area and sometimes even put great pressure on us to make concessions. The Soviet Union, on the other hand, though perhaps it does not want a war—especially one you will not win—does not desire peace, either. It wants to keep the kettle boiling, the better to manipulate you, and sell you its obsolete military hardware.

In the early 1970s Russia refused President Nixon's offer to jointly arrange a settlement, even though the United States was prepared to mediate such a settlement and, at a certain point, to impose it on Israel. The Soviet Union was not ready for that. Aren't the Russians the real villains in refusing the even longer-standing U.S. offer to observe a mutual arms embargo on all Middle East countries? Such an embargo might have prevented much of the bloodshed and forced us all to coexist—if not at peace, at least without recurrent wars.

The Russians don't give a damn how many Jews, how many Arabs die. They don't mind it at all if we go on building massive war machines instead of developing our own countries and our own peoples. Aren't they the real villains and we, Sana, the silly pawns and lackeys?

Hassan: We are both victims, Amos. We are both pawns of the global ambitions of the superpowers, who use us to achieve their own ends. Yes, I do think the Russians are villains. They would certainly not mind sacrificing us if it served their interests. They did that before the 1967 war when they egged us on by giving us false information that you were amassing troops for an attack on the Syrian front. They did it again in 1974 when they encouraged Syrian intransigence because they felt that a U.S.-sponsored peace settlement would cut them out of the area.

But the Russians are not the main villains, as you put it. The United States is equally villainous. I am very skeptical myself of the so-called moral interest of the

United States in its support for Israel. Where was this moral interest in the period 1948–1958, when the Israelis were crying out for arms and for admission into some defense pact? At that time the United States was deaf to your pleas because it was not interested in courting you. On the contrary, it was interested in courting the Arabs and inducing them to join a defense pact against the Soviet Union. It wanted to encircle the Soviet Union with American bases in Arab countries. Only after 1958, when the United States no longer needed Arab bases because of the development of long-range missiles, did the United States discover its so-called moral interest in Israel. And is not American support for Israel and for the conservative Arab countries designed to protect America's own sordid oil interests?

If you ask me if we would be better off without superpower interference, I would say yes if it would really mean a general embargo on arms for all sides. But I would say no if it meant that the Soviets would no longer be there to support us, and the United States would no longer be there to pressure Israel to make concessions. Then you could do what you please and present us with a peace settlement dictated on your own terms.

Elon: That is not at all what Israelis mean. If that's what you think they mean, you're stuck in your paranoia. What I am suggesting, Sana, is that we make real peace and at the same time free ourselves from being the pawns of the superpowers.

Hassan: As we perceive them, our fears are real. You may find it hard to believe that we could be afraid of you because there are so many of us and so few of you and because you are so conscious of your own fears of being thrown into the sea. But we are terribly afraid of being left at your mercy because we know that it is not the number of men but the organizational skill and technological know-how that determines the outcome of wars. We have never yet won a war against you, and your overwhelming military superiority makes us very anxious. We are afraid that without the restraining hand of a big power you might abuse your superior military power. But perhaps these fears are paranoic. I guess I too have been infected by the terrible suspicions and hostilities which divide us. You almost put me to shame. Forgive me . . . Release from big-power tutelage coupled with a real peace is certainly what I want. And perhaps it's what most Egyptians want too, although I know I would be hard put to convince you of that, since the Egyptian press often paints so fiercely different and so fanatic a picture of our feelings toward you.

Elon: Are you in fact saying, Sana, that the extremist Egyptian press is unrepresentative of Egyptian opinion?

Hassan: Yes, I am definitely saying that. I think that the press is always behind the times, if you like.

Elon: But it is a government-controlled press, and it reflects government opinion, doesn't it?

Hassan: It reflects but it does not actually express it. The Egyptian press generally adopts a much harder line because it is used by the government to placate the militants at home and to quiet opposition. The government tries to rationalize all the concessions we make to you by an-

nouncing in the press that these are not really concessions, that they are just stages of the struggle and tactical
moves.

Elon: And yet, in the absence of direct negotiations between
the Israelis and the Egyptians, the extremist Egyptian
press is the only thing most Israelis can go by. What alternatives do we have for a different assessment of the
Egyptian position?

Hassan: Certainly in the case of Egypt, you cannot argue
that the press is the only thing that Israel has to go by,
Amos. Right now, for example, there are many objective
developments which, if you only cared to look at them,
would point definitely to the fact that Egypt is preparing
for peace. Egypt has already proceeded to clear the Suez
Canal, even though she had originally stated that she
would not do so before the Israelis withdrew completely
from all occupied territories. Egypt is drawing up plans
for rebuilding the cities along the canal. She is investing
in those cities. If Egypt wanted another war, she wouldn't
invest all this money there.

Elon: Why not, Sana? Nasser leveled Egyptian cities to the
ground when it served his purpose; Sadat might do it
again.

Hassan: Amos, now it is you who are being paranoid. I've
already explained that the destruction of the cities was
not part of a premeditated plan by Nasser. In any case,
Sadat would surely not repeat Nasser's mistakes. There
are many other developments which you should bear in
mind. Sadat has turned himself into the guarantor of

Israeli good intentions, the salesman of U.S. policies to other Arab countries, such as Syria. This proves that he does have a stake in a peaceful settlement.

Look at the changing structure of the Egyptian elite. It is becoming quite conservative, interested in the return to a free-enterprise economy of which it will be the primary beneficiary. It is clear to these people that no Arab countries, and certainly no Western countries, or the Japanese, are going to invest in Egypt as long as the country is torn by war. So they have developed, at the very least, an economic interest in peace.

Elon: Well, I hope you're right, but your press still does worry me.

Hassan: You are right to criticize our press, but don't just read selectively what reinforces your own view. In the past few months there have been many articles in the Egyptian press deploring the continuance of the war and urging a peace settlement. Then, there was an exchange of letters between President Sadat's wife and an Israeli mother who had lost her son in the war, reprinted in *Al Mussawar* on March 7, 1974.

Elon: That letter was also reprinted in the Israeli press, probably one of the few instances when your papers and ours said the same thing.

Hassan: There are also many Egyptian intellectuals who are expressing a very genuine war-weariness. For example, Nagib Mahfuz, our foremost novelist, wrote two books after the '67 war, which deplored the war and its effect on the country. And Tewfik al Hakim, our most famous

playwright, published a monograph last year entitled
"The Return of Awareness," in which he deplored the
war. Let me read some of it to you:

"But we were not satisfied with two wars and two defeats—no, we had to have a third one! We don't know
exactly how many thousands of lives and how many thousands of millions of pounds we lost in this war, but if this
money had been spent on our villages, approximately
four thousand in number, each village would have gotten
one million pounds, enough to build it anew, to raise its
standards of living to that of a European village. But our
peasants have remained with their ignorance, disease and
their poverty. All these millions, which were the product
of Egyptian labor, have gone down the drain. On top of
that, we have suffered an atrocious defeat and five years
have gone by without war or peace during which Egypt
has stagnated. We have spent . . . enough money on war
to build the Aswan Dam twice over. What is this madness? What will history have to say about our revolution-
ary era?"

Elon: We may have more in common than we think, or sus-
pected. The content and tenor of modern Israeli literature express the same horror of war, the same desperate
striving for peace. This applies to every single major
Israeli novel of the past thirty years. But how do we
translate literature into politics? How are we going to
break the vicious circle?

You know what? Let's try an experiment. Why don't
you say what you would do if you were the Israeli Prime
Minister and truly wanted peace. Then I'll try to say

what I would do if I were the President and truly wanted peace with Israel.

Hassan: Well, Amos, what would you do if you were Sadat and truly wanted peace?

Elon: I would first of all recognize Israeli fears as very real and I would try to alleviate these fears of genocide and liquidation by formally recognizing Israel's right to exist as a sovereign state within secure borders, mutually agreed upon between the two of us. If I were President Sadat, I would proclaim Egypt's readiness to open a new era of peace and reconciliation. To make such recognition more effective, I would broadcast it directly to Israel and at the same time give it out in Arabic to the Egyptian public.

If you are right about the present situation in your country, then, I daresay, President Sadat could make such a declaration and be held as a courageous statesman by those elements in Egypt you said were in favor of peace with Israel. If that is what they want, they would only cheer Sadat for his statesmanship. It is often said that only the late President Nasser was big and courageous enough or charismatic enough as a leader to take such a step; but he, alas, is dead. Still, President Sadat could make such a declaration too. He would evoke enormous response in Israel, and elicit a readiness for far-reaching compromise.

It would have to be a very clear and straightforward declaration, not indirectly in the form of, say, a reference to the vague Security Council Resolution 242, which is interpreted differently, as you know, by the Arabs and by the Israelis, just as it is interpreted differently by the Russians and the Americans.

Now, Sana, couldn't President Sadat give us this proof? Couldn't he do this?

Hassan: First of all, he has already given ample proof. As we have discussed, in his acceptance of the Rogers peace plan, in his correspondence with Ambassador Jarring, and in his willingness to go to Geneva, he agreed to a peace settlement with Israel which would grant Israel de jure recognition.

Now, let me ask you: What kind of proof have your people given us of their intentions? Early in 1974, when the peace negotiations were just beginning, Mrs. Meir was saying that Golan is an integral part of Israel. And then she had the gall to act outraged when, a few days later, President Assad of Syria retorted that all of Israel was a part of Syria. The National Religious Front, which participated in the Israeli Cabinet, opposes the return of Judea and Samaria, which they view as part of Israel by "historical" right. In view of this, I think Sadat has done a lot. He wants peace and he says so openly.

As to broadcasting directly to Israel—yes, of course. that would be very nice. But this is the kind of final legitimization of Israel that he has to withhold until Israel is prepared to grant him a quid pro quo in the form of a return of territories. After all, it is the only trump card he has left.

Elon: Is it really? You make him sound so helpless. After all, he also has an army of half a million men. They did not do so badly in 1973.

I admit I consider Mrs. Meir's statement on the Golan Heights most unfortunate. I wish she had never made it. But can't you see, she wanted a *secure* border with Syria? It is not an unreasonable demand in view of past Arab threats and the relative vulnerability of the old border with Syria. She made these statements because you were still unprepared to give us even token proof of your intent. I completely agree, Sana, that the burden of territorial compromise lies with us. But the burden of proof that you intend to live in peace with us is on you. You started the wars, beginning in 1948; we did not.

Hassan: You still don't understand what I'm trying to convey to you, Amos. From your perspective, the initial act of aggression was ours, but from our perspective, the 1948 war was a defensive war. It was an attempt to gain back for the Palestinians what was rightfully theirs. I'm not condoning the corrupt King Farouk. He certainly didn't give a damn about the Palestinians, but many others did. From your perspective, you were just returning home. You were gracious enough to propose the partition of Palestine. You said to the Palestinians: "Move over, you guys! Leave us a little room!" But from our perspective, the Palestinians could hardly be expected to be grateful for your generosity in letting them keep half of their own house. For the Palestinians it was a situation, if you like, of Solomon and the two mothers. The real mother didn't want the baby cut in half.

Elon: But countries are not babies. And people must compromise somewhere.

Hassan: I, too, wish that we had been more considerate, more flexible. But you must understand that it was far easier for you to be conciliatory than it was for us, as the injured party, to be magnanimous. Unfortunately, it looked to us at the time as if the compromises you were asking for would be a Trojan horse that would one day destroy us. If you had just wanted a shelter, a refuge, a national home, we would have been glad to grant it, as we gave refuge to the Jews after the Spanish Inquisition. But we knew that the compromises you were asking for were just a beginning; you were aiming at the establishment of a state from which one day we would be excluded.

Because of this, we feel that it is up to Israel to prove that her intentions are innocent, that she has no further design beyond acquiring for the Jews, who have suffered so much in their history, a state of their own as a shelter. But every time there has been a war, in 1948 or 1967, you did not return the territory you conquered. You always say that the wars were provoked by us. Aren't you forgetting 1956? Then it was you who attacked, in alliance with two colonial powers, thereby giving credence to the worst of our fears—that you were just a spearhead of Western imperialism.

Of course I wish that Sadat would come out more openly and placate your fears, but you have to make it easier for us.

Elon: Sana, neither attack was ever justified. Neither your attack nor ours. Don't forget that in 1956, we did return the territory. Still, you did not make peace even then. The catastrophe is that no alternative to war was ever

found. The succession of wars continued. One disaster
followed another, generating new fears on top of the old
ones.

Our compromise proposal—halving the baby—was not
so unreasonable. In 1948 the United Nations resolved
that Palestine be partitioned. That resolution was not
predicated upon an abstract principle of justice. It was
based on a clear and deliberate choice against the great
injustice which would have ensued if no Jewish homeland had been set up. Partitioning the land between us
and the Palestinian Arabs was seen as the lesser injustice.
The partition resolution was based on an awareness that
for better or worse, two national movements had clashed
over the possession of Palestine, two rights, two kinds of
justice—the very essence, if you like, of high Greek tragedy. The baby does get cut up in Greek tragedy, Sana,
though not in the Bible or in the Koran. All this is very
ironical, for the tragic sense of life is alien to your Moslem
tradition, as it is to Judaism. In both, the righteous shall
be rewarded and the evil punished. Nevertheless, here
we find ourselves, in a most un-Moslem, un-Jewish Greek
tragedy.

I regret the 1956 attack, as I regret yours eight years
before. I deplore it all the more because it took place in
collusion with France and England and reinforced in the
minds of the Arabs the stereotype that we were part of
some grand imperialist design. We were cast into that
role almost against our will. It was said at the time in
Israel that when the British and French are your allies,
you don't need any enemies. But for God's sake! I know we

can't start from scratch, but we must do something to free ourselves from this tragedy.

Hassan: I think you're right, Amos. There is no question that this tragedy is the result of a clash between two rights. I believe that your claim is of equal moral validity with ours. And I fervently hope that the Arabs will one day come to see this. I deplore our lack of empathy, that we have not until now acquired this tragic sense of which you speak, that we have always tended to see things in black-and-white, to see ourselves as the victim and you as the villain. I am confident, however, that this sympathy will come.

You might say that there are three stages in our relationship with you. The first is the recognition that Israel is a fact, a reality, which we cannot destroy. The second is the recognition that it would be immoral for us to attempt to destroy it, even if we had the military power to do so, because it would cause so much bloodshed. And the third is to come to see Israel as intrinsically a good with a positive contribution to make for us and for all mankind.

I believe we are definitely at the first stage and we are moving along toward the second. With your help, we may one day achieve the third. It is not impossible that one day the Arabs themselves will be the Zionists. But the important thing is—can you find ways to help us?

Elon: What are the steps you would have us take?

Hassan: I would first of all stop the process of creeping annexation by announcing that in return for a peace settlement with the Arabs, I would be prepared to return all of the occupied territory, except what was absolutely essential to Israel's security.

Most important, you must declare once and for all that you would be prepared to see a Palestinian state set up on the West Bank and in Gaza. Your unwillingness to do this, thus far, has converted our struggle against you from a Pan-Arab involvement to a just war of liberation. It directly led to the war in '73.

Elon: Perhaps we both boxed ourselves into taking rigid positions that became self-fulfilling prophecies on both sides. The more wars *you* launched, the more aggressive, the more hateful, the more destructive you appeared in our eyes. And the more wars *we* won, the more expansionist and greedy for new territories we began to appear in your eyes. Now, if I were an outsider, a third party, I would probably be concluding at this point that we—you, Sana, and I—continue to be enmeshed in the myths and stereotypes that were generated on your side and on ours by the fears and threats of the past thirty years. But I am not an outsider, Sana, and neither are you. We both react out of our own pasts and from within our societies and cultures, not from without.

I think, therefore, that when you agreed before that we are not devils, as so many Arabs have thought in the past, you still somehow hold on to the belief that we should be angels. But we are not. We are frightened refugees and survivors from perhaps the greatest disaster that ever struck a single people in history. That's what we're like.

It makes us strong and weak at the same time. It makes us beautiful and ugly, but that's how we are. I don't believe that we really could have acted differently, or that others would have. At the same time, you are right in saying that we should not have begun a process of creeping annexation, as we did in Sinai or on the West Bank. We should have left everything open. We should have waited for you to come around. We acted under extreme provocation, of course, because we are human, and because in Israel, as in Egypt, politics is a game of power, pressures and counterpressures—and yes, a game of self-fulfilling prophecies too!

4

Israel and Syria

Hassan: Between Egypt and Israel, at least, there is a chance to change our relationship now.

Elon: Assuming that this is true of Egypt, what about the other Arab countries? Some of them are swimming in money and are courted by the old European colonialist powers, their previous oppressors. Aren't you afraid, Sana, that this new economic power, coupled with the Arabs' military achievements in 1973, will go to their heads to the extent that they will be even less ready than in the past to make peace? Or at least, start a process growing toward peace?

Hassan: No. The Arabs are well aware of the limitations of their own power. They know that they fought this war under the best of all possible circumstances and that many of these advantages—surprise attack, Soviet backing and Arab solidarity—may not repeat themselves.

Elon: Aren't they likely to tell themselves now, "We did pretty well in the war of 1973, certainly in comparison to 1967, 1956 or 1948. Next time we might do even better. Next time we'll move in for the kill and finish the whole business for all time"?

Hassan: Well, unfortunately, some of the vocal militants in the Arab camp are saying just this, but you must not have a monolithic view of the Arab. The situation is much more complex than that. I find it odd that you and everybody else are so mesmerized by the spectacular use of the Arab oil weapon and by the recent show of Arab unity. Some people are even talking about the Arabs as though they were a single and potent world power. Even Dr. Kissinger is reported to have warned the Israelis to settle quickly and get the best they can now before the Arabs become fully aware of the real extent of their power and international influence. Israelis, too, seem to swing from one extreme to another, as do many Westerners: from utter contempt of the Arabs, from a belief that they are forever doomed to disunity and impotence, to the magnification of Arab power beyond all realistic proportion. The oil is your opiate, and the opiate of the West much more than ours.

Elon: Still, the West is hooked on oil and you guys are the pushers. Surely not even the men in the Kremlin, in their most audacious dreams of glory, ever imagined that the medieval king of Saudi Arabia and the feudal sheiks of Kuwait and Abu Dhabi would help them to undermine NATO.

Hassan: There is more infighting among the pushers than you think. I agree that the oil weapon has been used very effectively by the Arabs. The friction which was generated between the United States and the European countries and among the European countries is quite self-evident. Equally obvious is the mad scramble among European countries and the Japanese to court our favor. Even the United States, for all its talk about not letting itself be blackmailed, has shown clear signs of nervousness.

But if you look beneath the surface of this United Arab front, you will see many signs of stresses and strains. It is much easier for each Arab country to come forward with a brief spurt of heroic effort than to sustain a common front over the long term. The Arabs realize that, and in a very large measure, it is the explanation for the genuine eagerness of many of the key Arab governments to settle the conflict through negotiations rather than to go to war once more.

Elon: But the short term is the truly crucial one, isn't it? Do you mean that the Arab dream of unity is dead, and that the internal stresses and strifes within the Arab world are now pushing you toward a settlement with us?

Hassan: The dream of Arab unity is still alive, but when one looks at it soberly, it is often no more than a mirage in the desert. Unity needs more than a dream to sustain it. It needs hard cash. The cash is in Saudi Arabia, in King Faisal's coffer. He is expected to accumulate up to fifty billion dollars within a very short period. Since 1967 the Egyptians and the Syrians have received several billion from Faisal. This money has been crucial to our war effort against you, just as without the Saudis, the oil weapon against you and the United States would not have been effective.

As a result, Saudi Arabia is now the key partner of the Arab war coalition. This is a new, unprecedented element. Without Saudi Arabia, the Arabs could not go on fighting wars against you, but Saudi interests are diametrically opposed to a prolongation of the conflict. Ever since the Saudi dynasty established itself in the 1920s, it has had a conservative perception of its interests. The Saudi dynasty wants above all to maintain the integrity of the country and to preserve its Islamic way of life. In their eyes, the real threats to their dynasty are Soviet Communism, Arab radicalism and Israeli Zionism. This has always been so and still is. Much as they hate Israel, the Arab-Israeli conflict places the Saudis in an embarrassing position vis-à-vis the United States. The Saudis realize that the United States is the main bulwark against Soviet Communism and a Nasser-style radicalism. In other words, the continuation of the Arab-Israeli conflict may cost the Saudi Arabians what they need most—U.S. support. Moreover, if the war continues, they will be expected to go on financing the Arab war effort, against Israel and, by implication, in alliance against the United States. They would have to at least match the current level of Israeli defense expenditure at a cost of several billion annually.

Elon: But couldn't they afford to pick up the tab?

Hassan: They may well be able to afford it, but don't forget that even though they are starting to buy arms from the United States, the bulk of their arms still comes from Russia. In fact, then, Saudi money is being used to help the Soviets entrench themselves in the area. Also, the total social and economic mobilization required to sustain the struggle against Israel helps the Arab radicals enhance their position in the area. This is exactly what the Egyptian Communists hope will happen and what the Saudis are afraid of.

In Egypt last year, the Communists were the most militant anti-Israelis. More than anyone else, they wanted an endless war against Israel which would lead to a general war of liberation. They were almost praying for Israeli troops to march into Cairo and get entangled on the way with the civilian population in the Delta area. They believed this would lead to a collapse of the government in the same way that the invading Japanese army helped generate the Chinese Communist revolution. This is the model they aspire to. It is exactly what the Saudis want to prevent at all costs.

The Saudis well remember that in 1966 Nasser, equipped with Soviet weapons, sent fifty thousand Egyptian soldiers to Yemen to help the Yemenite republicans topple the king. They are afraid that the same thing might happen to them. When the Saudis give money to other Arab countries, they can never be sure that that money won't be used against them. Nor can they simply withhold the money, lest they be accused of treason, once again possibly turning the people against the throne.

Contrast this with a situation of peace, where, instead of alienating the United States and entrenching the Soviets, instead of endangering their throne and their wealth, Saudi cooperation with the United States would no longer seem treasonable. Instead of putting Saudi money into the war effort, this money could be invested in the Arab countries. It would affect economic development, enhance the stability of the more conservative governments and reverse the trend toward radicalism, especially in Egypt.

Elon: You mean the King of Saudi Arabia, of all people, is the real pacifist among the Arabs today?

Hassan: Saudi Arabia is not the only member of the Arab coalition to oppose a prolongation of war against Israel. Kuwait and the other Arab sheikdoms share this same interest. All of these countries would welcome a peace settlement with Israel; and so, I believe, would Egypt. But the radical Arab countries would not. So you can see, the United Arab Front is not a union for all purposes. It is just a coalition of countries with conflicting interests joined together to achieve a specific purpose: to break the stalemate, to weaken Israel, to get the United States to pressure Israel for concessions. It sounds ironic, but in a sense, King Faisal really is Israel's ally today.

Elon: Really? I understand that his opposition to Israel is not merely political but religious. He hasn't even arrived at the Age of Nationalism; politically he is said to live in the Middle Ages. After his first meeting with King Faisal,

Dr. Kissinger—probably the first Jew ever permitted to enter Saudi Arabia—concluded almost in despair that he is "a religious fanatic." A few weeks later a group of French newspapermen visited Saudi Arabia. To enter the country they had to produce baptismal certificates. As a parting gift the King presented each with a copy of *The Protocols of the Elders of Zion*. And yet, Faisal wants peace? Are you saying, Sana, that King Faisal's money is dearer to him than his faith?

Hassan: Much as I hate to find myself praising such a backward regime, King Faisal, whom you call a medieval monarch, has acted far more cleverly than many modern rulers in this area, including your own. He is a crafty politician who clearly realizes the limits of his power. He knows how far he can go. He prevented a further hike in oil prices as demanded by the other oil producers and pushed for a lifting of the oil embargo against the United States. His hostility to Israel is certainly inspired by religious fanaticism. He is a Moslem fundamentalist. In his eyes, Jews like Christians, who do not believe in Allah, have an inferior religion. His view of the Jews is the traditional Moslem one, of condescension.

Elon: And contempt?

Hassan: No, not contempt. Perhaps disdain. He's outraged that the people who traditionally were a tolerated minority within the Islamic empire, now have the nerve to turn against their former benefactors.

Elon: It's like being blackballed by a club to which he did not want to belong in the first place.

Hassan: Well, it's not just religious fanaticism or a traditional sense of superiority. The more important reason for Faisal's hostility is that Israel has always been seen by the Saudis as responsible for the penetration of the Soviets into the Arab area. Faisal also thinks that the Arab-Israeli conflict has helped Arab radicals enhance their position in the Arab countries. He sees you as responsible for the spread of that godless socialism and Communism which he so hates. And, in a simple-minded way, he believes that U.S. support for Israel is due entirely to the sinister Jewish influence of crafty Jews in the bazaars of Wall Street.

Elon: His simple-mindedness isn't such a guarantee for peace as you seem to imply, Sana. For what is he going to do with his billions of new money? If he invests in capital goods, he is inviting revolution or the kind of social change through industrialization that will erode his absolute power. That's why he is investing so much of his money in arms, arms that he will surely use against us. I don't think he will want to let them corrode in the sun.

Hassan: He may be simple-minded, but his overriding instinct is survival. In the past, his sense of self-preservation has outweighed all his political and religious prejudices.

Elon: He's not the only Arab ruler with enormous amounts of money looking for ways to spend it profitably. There's Iraq, under a fanatically radical government and leaning toward the Soviet Union. And there is the peripatetic Colonel Gaddafi of Libya, of course. Both Iraq and Libya confirm the old established rule that the farther away from Israel an Arab country is, the more hateful its attitude, the more belligerent its policy.

Hassan: It is true that Libya and Iraq do not have a vested interest in peace as do the conservative oil sheikdoms. But I would not worry too much about Libya and Iraq. Iraq, as you know, is very much engrossed in her own internal problems, particularly in keeping the Kurds under control; she also has her hands full because of repeated clashes with Iran. She cannot commit large numbers of her troops to the Israeli front. As for the Libyans, they are too remote geographically and they do not have many troops to commit. The most they could do is contribute a few airplanes and money. If we could thresh out a peace settlement between the main contestants, I seriously doubt that Libya and Iraq could put spikes in the wheels.

Elon: Yes, if we only could. But although Libya is remote, it could still finance Syrian intransigence.

Hassan: It's true, Syrians are on the whole much more intransigent than Egyptians. Egyptians are often contemptuous of Syrians and regard them as humorless doctrinaires, cold-blooded bullies. Syrians, on their part, often decry us for our passivity and easy living. In a way, the Syrians are the Germans of the Middle East and we are the Italians—for reasons that are sometimes curiously similar.

When Egypt and Syria fused in 1958 to form the United Arab Republic, President Kuwatly of Syria warned

Nasser, "I am turning over to you six million rulers. May Allah help you."

In Egypt we are often Egyptians first, and Arabs second. The Egyptian identification as Arabs is of recent origin. It only dates back to Nasser. This is why Egyptian isolationism resurges whenever involvement in Arab affairs leads to a setback.

But the Syrians have always had trouble finding their own identity as Syrians. The country is a mosaic of ethnic groups and religious sects and conflicting regional loyalties. Syrians compensate for a weak sense of national identity by an extreme form of Pan-Arab nationalism. This is one reason why they are much more passionately involved in the Palestinian cause and in the "sacred war against the Zionist intruders." Another reason is the narrow power base of the ruling Baath party, and its internal factionalism. The President of Syria, even if he wants peace, is in a much weaker position than President Sadat of Egypt and therefore cannot be as conciliatory. For a variety of internal and historical reasons the Syrians think it's in their interest to maintain at least a low level of hostility with Israel.

Our great difficulty is that the future of peace in the area depends to an extent on Syria. The difficulty is compounded by the fact that—for reasons of their own—the Soviets have always encouraged Syrian intransigence by offers of diplomatic support and arms deliveries.

Elon: If peace really depends on the way Syria goes, aren't our hopes rather slim? Syria is governed by a fanatical fascist regime, which is often as cruel toward its own people as it is toward us. The Libyans and the Soviets don't have to exert themselves to sustain Syrian intransigence, or even brutality. Look how they treated our prisoners of war and their disregard for the fate of their own prisoners in Israeli hands. Caring little for their own POWs, they refused us even the names of ours, whom they tortured barbarically. And on the good will of such men we must depend?

Hassan: When you characterize the Syrians as you do—as "a fanatical fascist regime"—you really don't make enough effort to understand them, as most Israelis do not.

It is true that the problem of reaching a peace settlement with Syria is difficult. The security arrangements are so much harder to work out in the case of Syria than in the case of Egypt. There is no natural barrier here, as the Sinai Desert, and no space for extensive buffer zones and demilitarizations. Also, on balance, I'm sorry to say that the incentives for the Syrians to settle with Israel remain fewer than for the Egyptians. The Syrians can live without recovering the rest of the Golan Heights for a couple of years. The loss of Golan does not inflict on them the kind of financial hardship that the loss of Suez did on the Egyptians. Therefore, they are much less in a hurry to break the deadlock. They are quite capable of sitting around and doing nothing for a long time except engaging the Israelis in periodic scrimmages.

But Israel should be more sensitive to Syrian fears and security needs. Syria's territorial contiguity with Israel makes her feel much more vulnerable to attack than Egypt. Regardless of who started the provocations, the

Syrians have, in their turn, suffered a great deal at the hands of the Israelis. Certainly the Syrians were asking for trouble and provoking it by shelling Israeli settlements from the Golan Heights. Certainly one could not expect the Israelis to feel any sympathy when they, quite naturally, responded in kind. However, the Israelis overreacted with inordinately vindictive retaliation to such Syrian provocation. To minor provocation, they have answered with massive air strikes. Israel, in her hatred for the Syrians, seemed determined to bomb the hell out of them, dazzled by her new-found military power after the 1967 victory.

Elon: Sana, by your own description the Syrians behaved like a nasty little boy on a playground who hits another child and then complains that the other hit back too hard. If you act aggressively, you must expect the response, which you cannot regulate. You can't have it both ways.

Hassan: You must understand that the Syrians see their fate as far more closely intertwined with the Palestinians than do the Egyptians, because Palestine was part of Syria under the Ottoman Empire and because Syrians have thousands of Palestinian refugees living in their midst in cities like Damascus. Consequently, they have developed much more empathy for them than we have. Most Egyptians have never set eyes on Palestinian refugees, since they were isolated in Gaza, which was separated from Egyptian cities by the Sinai Desert. To the average Syrian the kibbutzniks below them, cultivating Palestinian lands, appeared as the spearhead of a growing Zionist population that would sweep through the hills of Golan and throw the Syrians out of their own land. I don't believe this. But even though it is a misperception, it is Israel's duty to deal with this fear and try to reassure the Syrians.

Elon: Do you mean to say that the very existence of the people in the kibbutzim, milking their cows, is seen as a threat to the military power of Syria?

Hassan: I know this seems ridiculous to you, as it does to me. But please try and understand them. Certainly you could find a more imaginative way of ensuring your own security than the blatant military occupation of Golan. I can understand that you would insist on a demilitarized Golan, under some form of patrol supervision, as a buffer between you and Syria. There is no doubt that in the case of Syria you have a real military problem. But you weaken your case by combining a military occupation with the establishment of Jewish settlements, as part of the colonization of those heights. If the military are there to protect the kibbutzniks below from the Syrian shelling, it makes no sense to set up new settlements on top of the mountains in the range of Syrian shelling. They feel you will soon need to take more land to protect these settlements, and this process of expansion will never end.

Elon: The longer you go on, the more you delineate the portrait of a paranoic frame of mind. I know you well enough by now, Sana, and refuse to believe that you share this irrationality yourself. But whether you share it or not, this is a very bleak picture you have drawn. It leaves little hope for peace with Syria.

Hassan: The picture is not quite as bleak as you see it, Amos. The Syrian elite is not of one mind. The more moderate among them want to encourage foreign investments, Japanese, Western and Arab, and to induce Syrian émigrés to return from Beirut and bring back some of their capital with them. Some of this has already begun to happen and a peace settlement would encourage investors even further. They must also fear the possibility, however remote, that Egypt will make a separate peace with Israel and leave Syria in the cold. And do not forget that the Syrians have at least accepted the Security Council Resolution Number 242, which commits them to recognize Israel in the context of a settlement.

They must also fear that the Soviets will not always, or unconditionally, support them. They must know that the Soviet Union has wider, global interests; it wants the benefits of a détente with the United States in terms of trade and investment. The Soviet Union must also fear that a Syria-instigated war resulting in another Arab defeat will cause the overthrow of friendly Arab regimes, thereby wiping out their position in the area. But I grant you that the Syrian situation is extremely volatile and I am less optimistic because the situation is relatively unpredictable.

Elon: "Less optimistic," Sana, is an understatement. You sound downright pessimistic, and to me the whole thing seems pretty grim. Why, then, is Egypt so dependent on Syria? Nasser himself once complained that the "crazy Syrians" brought him nothing but mischief. Why can't Egypt take a lead and make peace with us in the hope that Syria one day will follow suit?

Hassan: I doubt that Egypt could settle it alone. Respect for Arab solidarity is only one reason. It is hard for Egypt to leave Syria in the lurch. More important, Egypt knows that if she alone makes peace with Israel, the settlement will not last. Sooner or later she will become embroiled in another war between Israel and those Arab states that did not make peace. An isolated Syria will continue to fester until she has caused the conflict to flare up once again and will force Egypt to become involved, and many other Arab states as well. However much we may wish it, Egypt and Israel are not alone in the area. We can't write our peace treaty upon a *tabula rasa*. We all operate out of a variety of our interests, loyalties and memories, and the overriding influence of our pasts.

Elon: Oh, curse that past! Your past as much as ours. See how it holds us entrapped! See how it crushes the slimmest hope! I am almost at a point where I believe in blind forces. Life in the Middle East in the past thirty or forty years certainly enhances a dark fatalism. Aren't we all driven by forces vastly more powerful than ourselves?

Earlier in our dialogue, Sana, you mentioned the disastrous impact upon the Arabs of their cultural and political decline in the past two or three centuries, a decline which fanaticized them and made them see everything in black-and-white only. Now, surely the same could be said about the various tragic forces that have swept the Jews from wherever they were to seek a national renaissance in their ancient homeland. The generation of my grandparents responded to the anti-Semitic outrages in Europe in the latter part of the nineteenth century by seeking a national renaissance and a safe haven in the ancient homeland. The generation of my parents and my own generation still live under the traumatic impact of the Nazi Holocaust. I know that the Arabs can't be held responsible for Hitler, but as we Jews saw it, we were like a people drowning in a ferocious sea, trying to hold on and climb onto a life raft big enough to hold both Arabs and Jews.

Now, I know the fears and I know the passions that prompted the Arabs' refusal to grant us a place of our own. Syria, which, as you say, now holds the key to peace, is the most extreme expression of that refusal. I know these fears well and I know our own motives too. An irresistible force is colliding with an immovable body. I won't conceal from you my worst dreams—and I have those quite frequently—that unless there is a radical change in this situation, we are both heading toward an apocalyptic disaster.

Hassan: Personally, I don't agree with the common Arab position that they were made to pay for the crimes of European anti-Semitism. It is immoral and callous. We are all part of the same human race and we share responsibility for one another. Unfortunately, most Arabs don't see it my way. Is it blind forces? I don't know. Maybe the Arabs respond to the trauma of their own history as much as you do to yours, and miscast you in the role of the imperialist villain. But I don't believe in an apocalypse, perhaps because I'm not a Jew. I believe in free will. If you like, I'll say it the way Herzl said it: "If you will it, it is no dream." If we will it, there will be peace.

5

Growing Up in Cairo-
Growing Up in Tel Aviv

Elon: Sana, in the short time that we've been talking, we've discovered something about ourselves, if only our compatibility even in the face of mutual distrust and fear. Why only now?

Hassan: Because Arabs and Israelis never meet. There is no communication between our countries, not even the minimum of communication that existed between the Soviet Union and the United States during the worst of the Cold War period.

Elon: We're more in the position of Red China and the United States before they met at the ping-pong table.

Hassan: Well, here we have the chance.

Elon: Have you always felt the way you do now about Israelis? How did you grow up to see Jews?

Hassan: When I grew up in Cairo in the fifties and sixties, the word "Zionist" was a dirty word which was muttered under one's breath, like "sweat" or "sex" in a Victorian household. And "Israel" wasn't a word at all. We heard only of "occupied Palestine." We referred to your government as the "gangster regime of Tel Aviv."

I was born into the upper class. My family belonged to the political and social elite, and we all went to foreign schools and studied abroad at foreign universities. But that did not make any difference in the way we regarded you. Everyone I knew shared this view of you as demons and villains.

Elon: Did you know any Jews in Cairo, Sana?

Hassan: But of course! We had many Jewish friends. However, Jews and Zionists were never the same thing. Jews were people one met in Cairo and abroad, Zionists were a dark and menacing horde—the Jews who had turned bad. This belief was true even in the so-called upper class in which I grew up. It was a remnant of that cosmopolitan mosaic of languages, religions and nationalities which Lawrence Durrell described so beautifully in "The Alexandria Quartet"—sophisticated, rich, often frivolous —Egyptians, Italians, Greeks, Armenians, Arabs, Christians, Moslems and Jews. We grew up together in the same schools, we played in the same clubs, visited each other's homes, dated each other, and occasionally, even intermarried.

Yet, however tolerant and easygoing the atmosphere was within this unique milieu, it was still narrow-minded and fanatic in its utter repugnance of anything with regard to Israel or Zionists. I remember when I was eight, I was spending the summer in Geneva with my family at the Hôtel du Rhône. I made friends with a kind of old gentleman who used to play with me in the lobby. One day my aunt saw me with him and immediately drew me aside. She hissed in my ear, "Do you know who that man is?" I said, "Yes, he's very nice to me. He plays cards with me and gives me candy." "But do you know who he is?" she repeated. "His name is Daniel Cohen," I said. "Yes," she answered, "his name is Daniel Cohen, and he's a Zionist."

She meant to say that he was an Israeli, but she would sooner utter a four-letter word than intone that hated word I-s-r-a-e-l. Today it's all changed, of course, but back in 1954 this was quite common. "He is a Zionist," she said again. I remember shuddering. I did not know exactly what it meant, but I knew that it was something evil. I felt he had betrayed me. I never spoke to him again.

A few years later, as a teen-ager, I had a Jewish boyfriend in Alexandria—the son of an old Sephardic family. I had been dating him for a year. One day I waited in his house for him to come back from school. As I looked at his books on the shelves my eyes fell on a little notebook tucked between two French novels. I leafed through it and discovered that it was a collection of hand-written poems. They were dedicated to Zion and expressed his yearning for Israel and the Jewish state.

First, I was hurt and a little jealous. Here, he had a

secret love that he had not told me about. We had been so close and yet he had kept it from me, as a secret, as if he were not one of us. My second reaction was one of unease. I had always thought of him as an Egyptian, but obviously, he held himself separate from the rest of us, in a "Jewish world," from which I was excluded.

I felt like an accomplice to a crime. I kept quiet about it for weeks, brooding over the discovery. Then one day I confronted him: "Why didn't you tell me about it?" He answered, "I did not think you would understand." Like so many Egyptian Jews, he and his family had to leave the country after the '67 war and they are now in America.

What about you, Amos, did you know Arabs when you grew up in Tel Aviv? What did you think of them?

Elon: I grew up in the thirties in Tel Aviv, before the first Arab-Israeli war. We didn't think about the Arabs much. In school we were taught that the British were the main adversary. They ruled the country and it was from them we had to gain our independence. We had little if any contact with Arabs. The two societies lived totally apart. It was as impossible for a Jew to have an Arab girl friend, or vice versa, as I suppose it is impossible for me, at this moment, to go to Alexandria and spend a happy weekend as a tourist on my Israeli passport.

The reasons were largely political and partly social. Palestine in the 1930s was not Egypt of the 1960s. Most Arab women in Palestine were closely sheltered and never went outside except heavily veiled in black. I don't think I ever saw the face of a Moslem woman in my youth, except among fellahin women in the villages, though some upper-class Arabs in Jerusalem married Jewish women.

I remember my father once brought an Arab acquaintance home for dinner. Needless to say, he came alone. He kept his wife locked up at home. It didn't mean much to me except that I remember it was an Arab guest and I think I was more impressed by his red fez than anything else.

We thought that the Arabs were incited by the British to keep us all under better control. Tel Aviv was an all-Jewish town, but it bordered on Arab Jaffa. I remember the riots of 1936–1939. Suddenly barricades went up between the two adjacent towns. At night we would hear the shooting and the wail of ambulance cars collecting the wounded and the dead. We boys were warned to watch out for booby traps on the way to school.

I don't remember how my parents took it—they were veteran Zionists and had migrated to Israel for ideological reasons, but also for safety. And now they were in danger, just as their relatives were who had remained in Austria, by now taken over by the Nazis. In the late thirties, Jewish villages and urban centers all over Palestine were attacked by Arab guerrillas; the British authorities seemed incapable of stemming the tide of arson and bloodshed. The Arabs called it their "national rebellion." We referred to it as the "Arab disturbances." The Jewish population, though it was armed and maintained a clandestine militia, the Hagana, rarely retaliated but practiced passive resistance, à la Gandhi, in conformity with the deeply ingrained pacifist and socialist traditions of the early Zionist founding fathers. But I remember a mass funeral for Jews killed in the skirmishes. A politician compared the Arab rebels to Ukrainian peasants launching a pogrom against Jews. My parents shared this view and I don't remember meeting anyone who didn't.

From early childhood, then, I equated the Arabs with violence, dark and menacing, unfamiliar, devoted to almost carefree killing. I grew up with stories of horrible mutilations of the sexual organs of Jews in remote settlements entrapped by Arab rioters. Of decapitated corpses, bandied around by mobs running amuck in the streets. And yet, I don't remember associating this general impression with Arabs one met casually during peaceful lulls in the countryside, in streets and market places. It was a disembodied fear. I don't remember any hate—not in me, anyway.

But I do remember when I was eleven, I went through a terrible experience. Only a week before, a dozen Jews had been killed in Tel Aviv by a bomb planted by the Arabs in the street. Tension was in the air, and fear. I was walking home one evening when a Jewish mob grabbed a suspicious-looking man who turned out to be an Arab. He had a loaded gun in his pocket and the mob began to beat him mercilessly. Two Jewish policemen rushed up and made frantic attempts to free him and lead him off to a police station. By now the mob was running wild. One tall blond young man—I'll never forget his face—hit the Arab on the head with a wooden plank. He collapsed on the ground but the crowd continued to kick him. I think he was dead on the spot. The two policemen were helpless.

The curious thing is that I don't remember being

particularly shocked at the time by what I saw. Only weeks later it came back to me with horror. I had night-mares about it for some time. I later witnessed infinitely worse instances of Arab atrocities against Israelis—you can't even begin to imagine, Sana, how horrible these atrocities were. Yet the raw face of that tall tough blond brute is firmly imprinted in my mind. I can see it before my eyes now.

Hassan: How terrible, Amos. Are these the only kind of impressions you have of the Arabs?

Elon: I remember another experience ten years later. In 1948 I was in the army, in the Israeli War of Independence. There was a particularly hard battle against the Jordanian army, which had invaded western Palestine. The Jordanians had pushed forward as far as Lod Airport, some ten miles from Tel Aviv. The battle waged back and forth through the towns of Lod and Ramlah until on the third day, we finally drove them back. I remember riding into Ramlah in a jeep in the early-morning hours. The Arab inhabitants were leaving town. Thousands of people were taking off for the hills in the east with their children and their miserable little bundles. I can't say the Israeli forces, who had just entered the city, were discouraging them in any way, though I know that elsewhere this had been the case.

The populations of Lod and Ramlah were moving out in the hope, most probably, that they would soon come back on the heels of the victorious Arab armies. We, on the other hand, were glad to see them go, if only because they would hopelessly bottleneck the roads leading to

Lod from the main concentrations of Jordanian forces farther east in the hills. And yet, as I watched these people trail out, I felt that they might never be able to come back. I had no reason to hate or dislike them and I did not rejoice at their fate.

Years later a friend who had witnessed a similar scene told me that as a Jew he felt dutybound to empathize with these refugees. I don't remember feeling particularly "Jewish" at the time—in Israel we are rarely self-conscious in this sense. But I do remember that as I stood in the dusty main square, I had more than an uncomfortable feeling that these people were paying not only the price for their leaders' mistakes but also the price for our own resurgence as an independent nation. Ever since, I have not been able to free myself from a nagging sense of guilt and unease, a moral discomfort which increased as the years went by without a political solution. While we were building our state, the Palestinian refugees were hibernating in their wretched camps—it bothers me very much.

Hassan: Now that I know you, Amos, I can picture you standing there—it's so different from the picture Arabs normally have of Israeli soldiers in the 1948 war. We never think of Israeli soldiers as having a conscience at all, or feeling guilty. We are only told of the horrible massacre of women and children that some of your soldiers perpetrated in 1948 in the Arab village of Deir Yassin, near Jerusalem. We are fixated on that massacre. We've been so traumatized by it that it's hard for us to remember sometimes that Deir Yassin was an exception rather than a rule. We tend to think of Israeli soldiers not as humane, decent people but as marauding gangs of terrorists intent on wiping us out.

Elon: The massacre at Deir Yassin was decried at the time by most Israelis. And the perpetrators of that massacre were ostracized for years.

But let me come back to the Arab refugees of the 1948 war. I know there were many factors involved in the unnecessary prolongation of the Arab refugee problem from one decade to the next. The Arab governments certainly bear a great share of the responsibility both in the creation and in the continuance of the Arab refugee tragedy. But it has always disturbed me that however rapacious, however bloodthirsty, however violent the Arab governments may have been since 1948, I know we bear at least part of the responsibility. For this reason I would not, throughout these years, rent or buy one of the abandoned Arab houses in Israel, of which there are so many. Whenever I enter such a house, I have a feeling that it is haunted somehow and overcast by the shadow of another man's calamity.

Most Israelis don't feel this way at all, but some do, Sana. There are times when the guilt feeling I speak of strikes the very nerve center of modern Israeli culture. So many of the finest novels, poems and plays written by Israelis, especially those of the younger generation, reflect this agony in one way or another, not in obscure works by unknown underground writers, but in the poetry and the novels of our best writers and poets.

It is a feeling that grows as the years go by. Among

Israeli writers, intellectuals and university people, a persistent predilection for self-censure has survived the agonies of war and threats of annihilation from the Arab side. I am speaking primarily of a second- and third-generation phenomenon. It is not widespread, but where it hits, it often strikes, as I said, that very nerve center of culture. The intellectual roots of this phenomenon are probably older than Zionism or the sovereign state of Israel. They are probably embedded in a sensibility often identified with the Jewish temperament.

Hassan: Amos, I wish more Israelis felt the way you do, but even more than that, I wish that more Arabs knew that this is how you feel. It could break the monolithic stereotype we have of the Israelis.

Elon: Is there anything parallel to this attitude in Arab literature, Sana? Or in Arab intellectual life?

Hassan: Not in this form. Arab literature is still very different from yours. It is not marked by the kind of tearing, soul-searching quality which is often a hallmark of Jewish writing, though I suspect it is as much under the spell of nineteenth-century Russian literature as it is influenced by Jewish sentiments. The little I have read of modern Israeli literature reminds me of Chekhov.

Modern Arab writers are very different: either they hold you exclusively guilty for what has happened or else they may still be reluctant to even face you as a subject. I can hardly think of a serious Arab novel or play with an Israeli protagonist. Is this an accident? Perhaps at the bottom of their hearts the best Arab novelists know that there is a measure of truth on both sides, though they cannot yet bring themselves to admit it. I say this because, in another form, you may indeed discern a related current in Arab letters, in the works of Naguib Mahfuz and Tewfik al Hakim. If these writers do not yet grant you a moral case—as I do—their work at least postulates another morality, utter repugnance of all war and of the suffering it inflicts, and which it will continue to inflict mercilessly if the differences are not peacefully resolved.

Elon: Has this literature, Sana, had any impact on the development of your own thinking, vis-à-vis Israel and the Jews?

Hassan: Not exactly. It was many influences. I suppose personally I was always a rebel against authority. As a teenager, not atypically, I rebelled against established notions. One very important turning point for me came when I was sixteen. I won a school competition organized by the New York *Herald Tribune*, which brought me to America as the Egyptian delegate for a political youth forum.

Elon: Was that your first trip to America?

Hassan: No, I had been here before, but only as a child. At this youth forum I met an Israeli girl approximately my age, who had won the same competition in Israel. We got on very well on the personal level but whenever we met in public, either on television or on school panels to discuss the Arab-Israeli problem, we clashed terribly. At the time I knew very little about the Arab-Israeli conflict except for what I had read in the government pamphlets which were given to me by the Ministry of Information before I left for America. As a result, the Israeli girl seemed to me a blatant liar and a hypocrite. I felt that she was trying to cover up all the outrages that the Israelis had committed against us, by posing as the victim of rapacious Arabs who, having so much land of their own, were denying the survivors of Auschwitz a refuge on a little bit of their territory. Yet, because I liked her as a person and because she seemed to speak with such conviction and with such emotional fervor, I began to think that she couldn't be just a hypocrite—there must be something about which I was in the dark. I said to myself, "Maybe she really believes in what she says, or else she is terribly misled, or there is something that I don't know." So I got sufficiently provoked by this to ask a boy I had met at Princeton High School in New Jersey if he would give me a book on the history of the Jewish people. He gave me *Exodus*, by Leon Uris. That book moved me terribly. In fact, I cried myself to sleep practically every night while reading it . . .

Elon: I hope you won't be mad at me, but for heaven's sake, I should have thought that book would turn you off, not on. Ever since *Exodus* made the transition from book to movie, with all its two-dimensional characters intact, it has nurtured the most asinine image of the modern sabra as a kind of blond, blue-eyed goyish Jew with a submachine gun in his left hand and a Bible in his right. The real Israelis are not all like that, you know.

Hassan: Well, but for me it was very important because I was so tormented by these two opposite images battling within me, even if they were both exaggerated: on the one hand, the noble idealistic Israeli tilling his soil under conditions of extreme hardship and fighting for his life against incredible odds; on the other hand, the image I had grown up with of murderous Zionist gangs massacring Arab women and children. When I went back to Cairo I told my friends at school that they were all wrong. I had discovered another side which they didn't know about.

Elon: What was their reaction?

Hassan: They didn't believe me. They said that I had been a victim of the Zionist propaganda machine in the United States. But subsequently I was influenced by many other books. Perhaps the ones I remember best are Elie Wiesel's books *Night* and *Dawn*; the taped interviews with Israeli soldiers, *The Seventh Day*; your book the *Israelis*; and Arieh Eliv's *Land of the Heart*. They showed me a face of Israel which I had never seen before. I was reading Wiesel just as the 1967 war broke out.

Elon: How did you feel at that time, in the weeks that preceded the war of 1967, when Nasser was massing troops in the Sinai, blockading the Gulf of Aqaba to Israeli shipping, and kicking out the United Nations emergency forces from the Sinai Peninsula?

Hassan: I hated what he did. I thought that he was just trying to show off to the other Arab nations. It was a silly display of *machismo*.

Elon: Did you say that to other Egyptians?

Hassan: Yes, I did. But they didn't agree. They felt that it was our legitimate right to close off Aqaba to Israeli shipping.   After all, they said, we are at war with Israel. No country at war can be expected to open its territorial waters to its enemy, and in fact, Israel had acquired access to the Gulf of Aqaba in the first place through an act of war in 1956.

Elon: And after the war—did your feelings change? As an Egyptian, did you suffer from that defeat?

Hassan: I was, naturally, torn between many feelings. When the war was going on, I hoped desperately that we would win. Afterward I was shocked by the humiliating defeat that we had suffered at your hands, the destruction of our entire military machine, the loss of Sinai and the Suez Canal.

And I was surprised by my feelings. I had always considered Nasser a fraud and had longed for his overthrow, but I suddenly found myself almost crying as I listened to his resignation speech over the radio. I felt I was personally humiliated; not just Nasser had been put to shame, but we had all been humiliated, as a nation. Not only had you won so easily, but you even got what you had always been after—Nasser's head as the ultimate trophy of your victory. Although I disliked Nasser, I wished he would take back his resignation in order to deny you this final triumph. Did you feel triumphant when Nasser resigned?

Elon: Did I feel triumphant? On that day I was in an armored troop carrier opposite Ismailia on the east bank of the Suez. We listened to Nasser's speech on a transistor radio. I was one of six or seven reservist soldiers in the armored vehicle who had been called up to active duty only two weeks before.

Hassan: My God! You mean you were there, Amos? That's terrible. You could have gotten killed!

Elon: Well, yes, Sana, that's what I meant to say all along. We weren't just faceless robots fighting one another, you know. Real people were involved, like you and me, and many got killed.

Hassan: I know that, but before, it seemed abstract. Now I have met you and the bare facts are real and very disturbing. I'm sure I'm not expressing myself well, but I feel that very strongly. For the first time, I feel guilt—as an Arab.

Elon: Sana, dear, how beautiful that you can say those words.

Hassan: It is a hard thing to admit, but I'm not ashamed to say it to you. I feel you understand.

Elon: Well, let's return to Nasser's resignation. As we were sitting there in the armored carrier, one man pulled out a flask and offered us all drinks to celebrate our victory. I suppose I felt rather elated. I was relieved like everybody else that the war, which I feared would cause tremendous casualties and possibly the destruction of Tel Aviv and other population centers, had ended in such a stupendous victory. I suppose I even leered at Nasser's demise—I never hated anybody as violently as I hated Nasser in the three weeks before the actual breakout of the war.

Although we were victorious, I considered that war then, and I still consider it today, a terrible calamity. You see, a few days before the war, when I was already in the army, I wrote an article for *Haaretz*, the Tel Aviv newspaper I worked for at the time. I urged the Israeli government to leave no stone unturned in its effort to resolve the crisis. I wrote that the war, whatever its outcome, would create even bigger problems than those it was trying to resolve. The article was delayed a day or two for purely technical reasons. In the meantime the war broke out, and the editors decided to shelve it.

Four weeks later, when I returned to the office after the war, the editor told me, "Aren't you happy your article was delayed? It was a stroke of luck for you. If it had appeared in print, you would look very foolish now in view of the great victory which we scored."

I don't remember whether I felt lucky or unlucky, but I do remember that despite the great victory, I understood that the war had probably been a disaster. It had broken a relatively long period of gradual disengagement between Egypt and Israel, when Israel was governed by the moderate, conciliatory, humane Levi Eshkol—a man of peace and compromise, if ever there was one—when Egypt had seemed to be busy elsewhere. If only that period could have lasted longer, if only it could have been permitted to mature! Nasser's war had wrecked it all. And it solved nothing. The war forced Israel to overextend itself territorially, and it bred the arrogance and cockiness that are now held responsible for our setbacks in 1973. On the other hand, it fanaticized the Arabs, and above all, the Palestinians, because of the humiliations we inflicted upon them.

Hassan: It was a disaster. I think I said before that I wanted Egypt to triumph. I shared with everybody else the humiliation of her defeat, but I thought that the '67 war was our fault. We brought this disaster upon ourselves.

Most of my friends disagreed with me. They felt that you knew all along that Nasser was just bluffing and did not really intend to go to war against you. The Egyptians felt that you used Nasser's bluff as a pretext to attack us in order to seize more of our territory. I think I said before that I felt Nasser was guilty of *machismo*. I confess I was ambivalent even then. I disagreed with the closing of the Gulf of Aqaba. I knew that by closing the strait, Nasser was forcing a war. On the other hand, I, too, felt it was outrageous of you to insist sanctimoniously that you had the right of free passage in our waters. It seemed to me, as it did to most Egyptians, that we had a perfect right to deny access to the gulf, since we were at war with you.

Elon: Did you really think that? You remind me of a character in an old Jewish anecdote who killed his father and mother. Later on, in court, he pleaded mercy because, as he said, he was an orphan.

Hassan: And your story reminds me of an Egyptian parable which circulated in 1967 during the war. A man murdered his friend in cold blood and then, at the funeral, was the one who cried the loudest. You see, to us it seemed ironic that you were faster on the draw, and then posed as the victims of our aggression.

Elon: I suspect that it is possible to exchange anecdotes like these endlessly. And you know? It might even do us some good.

Hassan: For months after the Six-Day War, I was tormented by all sorts of conflicting feelings. I read reports in the French press that Israeli officers had forced Egyptian soldiers to walk barefoot through the scorching desert sands. Their feet were bleeding and they were dying of thirst, but they were refused water by Israeli officers.

Elon: I don't know if this really happened. I never saw anything like it. In fact, I saw the opposite: Israeli soldiers sharing their last water rations with Egyptians who were struggling through the desert, looking for someone to surrender to. Or, I saw Israeli helicopters scanning remote crags and crevices for wounded Egyptians in order to evacuate them to a field hospital.

But if I never saw what you described just now, that doesn't mean it didn't happen. War inevitably brings out the worst in men. In us, and in you. Do I have to tell you horrors committed by Egyptian or Syrian soldiers, or Palestinian guerrillas? We also commit horrors. I saw some awful things myself. I was horrified at one point when I saw the crew of an Israeli supply truck taking pot shots at Egyptian stragglers just for the fun of it. You agreed before that we are not devils. Why do you go on assuming, Sana, that by the same token, we must be angels?

Hassan: I suppose I still feel that you must. I know this is absurd, but somehow it upsets me less to hear that American soldiers have committed massacres like My Lai than to hear that Israeli soldiers have committed atrocities. It's ironic that I should expect higher ethical standards of my own enemies than I do of other nations. You see, it's so difficult for an Arab to wrest herself to the position that I take, to see your moral case as valid. Once I do that and publicly put myself out for the other side, and suffer much criticism and ostracism for that reason, I guess I expect to be rewarded by your exemplary behavior. Perhaps it is naïve and unrealistic, but it's so much easier for an Arab to make the case for a perfectly moral Israel than for one that is merely human. I have never been in a war myself. Perhaps it would bring out the worst in me too. I feel ashamed in a way to be preaching to you, who have gone through it all and emerged from it without hatred. For God's sake, that's why we must end this war and make peace before we all turn into animals.

6

The Palestinians

Hassan: As you know, Amos, prejudice, stereotypes and ignorance are by no means the only obstacles to peace between us. A far more important hindrance has been your rigid thinking on the question of the right of the Palestinians to be a nation. On this point, Israel's attitude has been absolutely callous and immoral. I say this because the politicians of Israel and Egypt and Jordan are quite capable of sacrificing the Palestinians to their own narrow interests. They may well sign a slip of paper which they will call peace. But a lasting peace and a true reconciliation between Arabs and Israelis is possible only if you recognize the rights of the Palestinians to self-determination.

Elon: Undoubtedly this is the very core of the problem.

The Arab-Israeli conflict started as a civil war between Palestinian Arabs and Israeli Jews. If it ever ends, it will have to end between Palestinian Arabs and Israeli Jews.

But you said "callous," Sana, and that is wrong. It was not just callousness on the part of the Israeli leadership that caused it in the beginning to ignore the possibility that the Palestinian Arabs may be as anxious as they are for national revival. Here too, I think, we should look beneath the surface. Please don't forget the different time sequence and the true order of prior events. When the first waves of Zionist settlers arrived in the country, there was little if any trace of Palestinian nationalism. Arab nationalism at the time was centered in Syria and in Egypt. Its stage was a vast area stretching from Baghdad in the east to Egypt in the west. Men of moderation like Weizmann or Ben-Gurion assumed that the national sentiment of the Arabs would focus on Baghdad, Mecca and Damascus, that they would find a natural and complete satisfaction in a proposed Arab kingdom centered around these historic sites.

At the time, this was much less improbable than it would seem today. The early Zionists were not callous or blind. They truly believed in the possibility of an Arab-Jewish compromise. They were men of peace. Perhaps they were naïve in believing that they could scramble eggs without breaking them. For a long time they favored a binational state. Events caught up with them as well as with you, and Zionism almost unconsciously became the midwife of Palestinian nationalism. In the process, everything got enmeshed in violence and stereotypes. Everything was complicated by power rivalries in the area and power rivalries in the world, rivalries which have very little to do with either Palestinian Arabs or Israeli Jews.

Hassan: In using the term "callous" I was not referring to the early Zionist settlers, who were undoubtedly well-meaning. In fact, I would regard a man like Weizmann as downright noble. The most I would accuse them of is moral myopia or naïve Utopianism.

I am speaking now of the recent past and the present conditions. I refer to your former Prime Minister, Golda Meir, who sanctimoniously pretended that there are no Palestinians at all. She was echoing certain early Zionists who pretended that Palestine was an empty land so that they would not feel guilty for displacing its native population. And although she herself led a nation of refugees, she was oblivious to the million Palestinians who had lost their homes as a consequence of your national resurgence. She consistently refused to allow them a state of their own. She declared time and again that she would not tolerate another Arab state, in addition to the four already on her borders. She often complained that Arabs regarded Jews only as a people, not as a nation, and attributed this attitude to the Arabs' peculiar mentality. It is a tragic irony that she did the very same thing to the Palestinians.

Perhaps I'm wrong to expect that your people, because they have suffered so much, should be the most capable of empathizing with our suffering. Perhaps people who suffer are so engrossed in their own miseries that they are the *least* capable of empathy. Approximately thirty thousand Palestinians have died so far in their struggle for nationhood. Surely this is proof enough of how badly they want to be a nation. And here is another irony: just as the Arabs ignored the fact that you fought four wars and were ready to die for your country, so you ignored the fact that the Palestinians were ready to do the same for theirs.

Elon: Sana, I never defended Mrs. Meir on this point and will not do so now. Anyway, we have a new government now. Still, I would very much like you to see that other factors were at work besides Meir's insensitive old age and the unimaginativeness that came from staying too long in power. As we have already discussed, Mrs. Meir led a harassed people which came into its own under convulsive circumstances that had not been imagined by anyone. What was planned originally as an orderly exodus from Europe became, in the end, a desperate escape from the death camps and gas chambers of Auschwitz.

Golda Meir arrived in Palestine in the early 1920s. Like so many of the early Zionists, she dreamed of a veritable golden future for Arabs as well as Jews, through education, social welfare, large-scale economic development and rising living standards. But wherever she turned, as a common laborer on a commune, or later as a trade-union functionary, or later still as a prominent politician, she encountered only bitter Arab hostility and violence, and utter refusal to hear of any compromise. Shortly after she arrived, the first bloody skirmishes occurred in the Arab rebellion of 1921, then again in 1926, in 1929, in 1936, and so on, and so on.

By the time Israel was carved out of the debris of the

British mandate in 1948, there was even less opportunity
for Meir to meet Palestinians except in violence and war.
On the eve of the first Israeli-Arab war of 1948 Mrs. Meir,
disguised in the veils of an Arab woman, made a last-
minute trip to Amman in Jordan. She met the then King
of Jordan, Abdullah, and pleaded with him to resolve the
conflict. Abdullah simply answered, "This is no time for
peace, this is a time for war." He sent her home and his
army in her wake to invade Palestine.

Meir's entire political outlook was shaped by these
experiences. They have made her hard and suspicious. I
once went to see her with a group of Israeli writers to
plead for some Arab villagers who, we felt, had been mis-
treated by the government. Amos Oz, the novelist, spoke
of peace and reconciliation, and called out to Mrs. Meir,
"Madame Prime Minister, don't you ever dream?" She
retorted, "I'm afraid to. My dreams, they wake me up at
night . . ."

We certainly bear a great responsibility for the fate of
the Palestinian-Arab refugees. I am sure most Israelis
would like to act upon that responsibility within the
framework of a peace settlement. But, Sana, don't the
Arab states bear a measure of the responsibility as well?
Instead of absorbing the Palestinian refugees, they locked
them up behind barbed wire in dismal tents and called
in the United Nations to support them at ten cents a day.
The Palestinian-Arab refugees were not the only refugees
who lost their homes in the upheavals that followed
World War II. There were at least fifty million refugees
in the world then, and most of them have subsequently
been settled and absorbed. Imagine, Sana, the state of

the world today if the Indians or Pakistanis or West Germans had behaved like the Arabs—if, instead of absorbing almost fifty million refugees, they, too, would have kept them festering in wretched refugee camps. But that's exactly what the Arab states have done since 1948.

Hassan: You should not really be making this kind of argument, Amos. It's shocking. It reminds me of Leonid Brezhnev, who once scolded the Jews for raising such a fuss about their six million dead. After all, he argued, over twenty-five million Russians and Poles had been killed by these same Nazis. It is true that there have been millions of Indians, Germans and Vietnamese refugees in the past thirty years who have been absorbed, but that does not make the suffering of one million Arab refugees any less poignant.

Elon: God! You're quite right here to chastise me. I've been making this argument for years, and it never occurred to me that it was really morally indefensible. Forgive me . . . But even so, Sana, don't you agree that the Arab states share a part of the responsibility for the Palestinian tragedy? I don't want to lighten our burden but simply to put the record straight. The leaders of the Arab states don't really give a damn about the Palestinian people. They simply use them to further their own sordid designs of power and influence.

Hassan: Perhaps they don't give a damn, but I do. Some Arab governments have undoubtedly used the Palestinians as pawns, but this is not the whole story, Amos. First of all, the Palestinians themselves do not want to be inte-

grated. They want to return to Palestine. No Arab government has a moral right to compel them to become integrated
against their will. You talk about the Arab governments
not doing anything to alleviate the plight of the Palestinians. You have to realize that as destitute as the Palestinians are, their conditions still compare favorably with
the miserable conditions of the Egyptian fellah and his
Syrian counterpart. The Jordanians themselves live off an
American pittance, and the Lebanese must export a
significant number of their own population in order to
maintain even the living standard which they now have.
As for the oil-rich Arab countries, they have absorbed a
significant number of the Palestinians. The Palestinians,
in fact, provide much of their present educated stratum.
The Kuwaiti, for example, have absorbed over one hundred thousand Palestinians, in a population of fewer than
seven hundred thousand.

There is, moreover, a general feeling among all Arabs
for the justice of the Palestinian cause. It is intense and
real and deeply felt. Even if some Arab rulers have used
and misused these feelings for their own personal glory
and personal ambition, it does not make these feelings
any less real. You, above all, should be able to understand
that. It is similar to the intense emotional commitment
which Jews in the Diaspora have for Israel. Just as they
feel that the establishment of Israel corrected a historical
injustice to the persecuted, homeless Jews, so do Arabs
feel that the establishment of a Palestinian state would
correct an injustice perpetrated against the Palestinians.
Now, I definitely want Israel to survive, but I want to put
an end to Palestinian homelessness in a way which

achieves for them a stable national identity without infringing upon yours. Whether there was or wasn't a Palestinian national identity sixty years ago, when the first band of Jewish settlers arrived in Palestine, is irrelevant. There was one well before the establishment of the state of Israel in 1948. The Arab rebellions of 1922, 1926, 1929 and 1936, which you referred to earlier, were but so many testimonials to the stirring of a national consciousness among the Palestinians. Those Israelis who would like to deny the existence of the Palestinians today should ask themselves against whom they were fighting during those years prior to the existence of the state, if not Palestinians. There *is* a national identity now. That is what matters. Fifty years ago, most people denied your claim to a national identity and a state of your own. You say that the Arab governments don't give a damn for the refugees. Does your government give a damn for the refugees? I suspect that it's not just solicitude for the refugees that makes Israel insist on our absorbing them. I suspect that they would like to see the refugee camps disappear so that Israel can forget about the Palestinians and not have to do anything for them.

For all of your government's criticism of our handling of the refugee problem, it did very little for them in five years after the 1967 war, in which the refugees were under Israeli jurisdiction in Gaza and the West Bank.

Elon: Naturally, the Israeli government would like the Palestinian camps to disappear. Of course it cares less about Arab refugees than about the million Jewish refugees we absorbed in our own country and to whom we gave a new dignity and a relatively decent new existence. The Arab governments didn't show this concern for their own people, for their own refugees. This is what I am suggesting. They have billions and billions of dollars in oil revenue, and yet, the Saudi Arabian contribution in 1973 to the United Nations fund for the support and reconstruction of Arab refugees was a mere $300,000. That's less than their king spends on gilded air-conditioned Cadillacs. Thus, he condemns these refugees to continue their lives in misery, in disease and in frustration.

Hassan: King Faisal could certainly spend his billions on better causes. The Palestinian refugees are one such cause. I for one wish he would spend as much money on them as he does on Fatah guerrillas and on Egyptian arms. We deserve a great part of the blame. We should exert ourselves more, get the refugees out of the camps and give them a new life. But taking them out of their dismal camps and even putting them into air-conditioned new luxury apartments, without letting them find their identity as a nation, isn't going to be enough.

Elon: Of course it's not enough. I fully understand that the Palestinian Arabs now feel as a nation. Like the Jews in the past, their national identity is heightened by misery and alienation, by the notion of living in a kind of diaspora, and the powerful myth of a lost homeland to be regained. This is why, in return for a peace treaty, I would like to see Israel withdraw from the West Bank and Gaza, on condition that these areas be demilitarized. The fact that partition broke down once, in 1967, does not mean we should not try it again, for practical reasons as well as on moral grounds. When two rights clash over possession of the same piece of real estate, the only just and practicable solution in the long run is to partition that piece of real estate between them.

Let's repartition the country once again. Not as between 1948–1967, when we were sealed off from one another by mine fields and barbed wire and hate and abysmal fears, but on different premises, in a mutual recognition of national and territorial rights and sovereignty. Within their part of the country the Palestinians should determine their own fate, their own identity. If they want to set up a Palestinian state, it's all right with me. If they want to be Jordanians or Ruritanians, it's all right with me too. If they want to join a larger Arab federation, or link up on a confederate basis with Israel, it's all right with me too. They should determine that for themselves. They should have the full right of self-determination.

Hassan: Well, if that's the way you feel, Amos, why doesn't Israel take the first step right away? Israel is the controlling power on the West Bank and in Gaza; there are over a million Palestinian Arabs there. Why don't you let them take their fate into their own hands and set up a state there and now?

Elon: But wouldn't that be self-defeating, really? As long as there is no formal peace with Jordan and the other Arab countries, wouldn't such a Palestinian state be set up, as it were, on Israeli bayonets? You might find a few sheiks on the West Bank who would go along with it and assume all sorts of highfalutin roles and titles, but the majority of Palestinians on the West Bank and abroad would be right to distrust an Israeli-sanctioned Palestinian puppet state. When the Moslems and Hindus divided the Indian subcontinent in 1947, India did not set up Pakistan for the Moslems, but each people built its own state within its allocated area. Economic and cultural cooperation is another matter: if the Palestinians feel they need technical assistance and economic support, Israel should give those readily. But I would hate to see Israel paternalistically setting up a Palestinian puppet state. If they want a state, the Palestinians should set it up on their own, after Israel withdraws and the peace settlement is signed.

Hassan: I still believe that you must take the first step. I understand that you don't want to be put in a paternalistic position, but you have to do something. It is you who scrambled the eggs in the first place, and now you have to help us separate them again. You can't wash your hands like Pontius Pilate. Let your government make a unilateral public declaration and say what you have said just now: that the Palestinians are entitled to determine their own fate, both on the West Bank and in Gaza—in whatever form they like. You must do that to encourage the Palestinian organizations, to help them break out of their cycle of despair. Up until now you have refused to recognize the Palestinian organizations as fit to talk to. Instead, you have always insisted on dealing only with the royal Jordanian government, a conservative bulwark in the area. It may be convenient for you, in the short run, to deal with King Hussein, but how can you expect

Hussein and his henchmen, who have massacred the Palestinians and repressed them since 1948, to make a fair settlement on their behalf? Furthermore, Hussein will one day vanish from the scene, but the Palestinian people and their problems will remain. Sooner or later other Arab nations will be embroiled once more in a war on their behalf. You must negotiate with the true representatives of the Palestinian people.

Elon: I would like to. But, Sana, where are they? Are they ready to recognize Israel? Are they ready to deal with us now even to the point where they will agree to let us put them in charge of the West Bank and Gaza? Who are they? The Black September people who perpetrated the massacre at the Olympic games in Munich? The Popular Democratic Front for the Liberation of Palestine, which staged the massacre of schoolchildren in May 1974 at Ma'alot in order to deliberately disrupt, as they put it, the Geneva peace talks?

Their formal program remains the total dismantling and destruction of the state of Israel and its people. Should we deal with Yassir Arafat, who heads Al Fatah and the Palestine Liberation Organization? Arafat and the PLO, in their solemn covenant of 1971, announced that Israel must be liquidated. The covenant of 1971 remains the official program of all Palestinian organizations. It not only calls for the destruction of Israel as an independent state but demands also that ninety percent of all Israelis pack their suitcases and go back to where they or their forefathers came from. Only those Jews could remain in the country who lived there in 1916. Don't you think the

Palestinians would have to change their "covenant" first? That a different, more constructive Palestinian leadership must emerge before the Israeli government can approach it with constructive offers?

Hassan: The massacre at Ma'alot was morally deplorable. But the answer to Ma'alot is not more Israeli retaliations in Lebanon and the death of more civilians—this time on the other side of the fence. I understand your difficulties in dealing with these people, but we cannot wait for a constructive leadership to emerge. The longer you wait, the more Black Septembrists will be born in tomorrow's refugee camps.

Your policy has been wrong, don't you see? You have continued to do what the British did before you: dealing only with the most reactionary elements, who do not represent current economic and social realities. By prohibiting political activity on the West Bank, you prevented the emergence of a new leadership, as an alternative to Arafat. By refusing to deal with the PLO, you acted as so many powers in the past, as the Americans acted toward the Viet Cong, the French toward the FLN in Algeria, and the British toward the Mau Mau. But even so, in the end the British understood what true statesmanship required. They made it a policy, in countries like Kenya, to take terrorists out of prisons and make them prime ministers. Need I remind you, Amos, that many states today, including your own, have at some time been governed by one-time terrorists?

Elon: This is unfair, Sana. You can't compare the Israelis within their own land to the French and British in their old colonies. But no matter. I agree that it is important to deal with the Palestinian terrorists even though their hands are soiled with blood—if only they were prepared to deal with us and recognize our right to exist as a sovereign state. The trouble is that they are not; their terrorist activities are avowedly aimed at disrupting the peace talks rather than at participating in them. It is childish of you to expect us to "make them prime ministers" or to expect that they will agree to let us appoint them to such office.

Hassan: I do not mean to be unfair in comparing Israelis to colonialists. One cannot call you colonialists yet, but I would not, if I were you, Amos, dismiss so lightly the possibility of the present situation evolving along colonial lines. The danger arises from the very nature of your occupation of the West Bank and from the settlements which you have set up there. There are many precursors of colonalism in the present situation, which even prominent Israelis find degrading. The Palestinians on the West Bank have no political rights whatsoever. There is an increasing use of Arab laborers, who are underpaid in comparison to the Israeli labor. Many of these people end up sleeping in streets and in stables. The discovery of these conditions even causes scandals in the Israeli press.

It is true that the Israeli government has provided Palestinians with work, has raised their standard of living and granted them free access to Israel. This in itself is an achievement. But I admire Israelis who are not content with this and who go on to demand more of their own government. I only wish that you would go even further and ask your government to come to an agreement with the PLO. Liberals like yourself are still afraid of them and only the left in Israel is prepared to deal with the PLO.

Elon: Whatever you may say about the Israeli occupation regime, I believe that it is probably the most humane foreign occupation in recent history. Even so, I don't want us to be occupiers, however humane. I want to put an end to the occupation of the West Bank. I want Israel to remain a country with a Jewish majority. I do not wish us to become the overlords of a million Arabs. I fear the corrupting influence upon Israel, the continued occupation of the West Bank. If this occupation continues, we will cease to be a democracy. That is why I want us to get out of there, but if the PLO wants to set up a state, they must first agree that they want to live in peace with us.

Hassan: I grant you that the PLO covenant of 1971 is hardly reassuring. It was formulated by a desperate people and is as much a disaster as was the Munich massacre. Furthermore, it is a ridiculous proposal which would allow hawks like Ezer Weizman and General Sharon to live in Palestine—because they are native-born—but evict doves like Liova Eliav, Abba Eban, Pinchas Sapir and Yitzhak Ben Aharon simply because they were born in Europe.

Elon: If the men and the policies of the PLO are disastrous and ridiculous, as you say, will you agree, then, that we don't really have anyone to talk to?

Hassan: No, I don't. Even Yassir Arafat has slowly been changing his position, as have many of the men around him. There have been strong pressures on the PLO to become more moderate and to tone down its demands. Both Egypt and the Soviet Union have urged it to form a provisional government that would represent a Palestinian state composed only of the West Bank and Gaza. In order to encourage the PLO to do this, Egypt has even renounced her sovereignty over Gaza. The PLO was not ready to change its position immediately after the October war. In fact, the PLO announced that it intended to continue the struggle for the liberation of *all* of Palestine. But since then, several of the resistance leaders, like Arafat of Al Fatah, have in general argued that the world is changing and that they can't afford to isolate themselves. They now display an unprecedented flexibility, in order to gain recognition for the PLO as the sole representative of the Palestinians. They insist that the West Bank be restored to them, not to Hussein. After that, they hope to continue the struggle by other means, by playing on the contradictions within Israeli society, joining hands with the progressive forces within Israel, and so forth.

Elon: I see little reason to believe the PLO is changing. Any softening in its public statements is mere rhetoric, a tactic designed to obscure what they really want—our total destruction.

Hassan: But even if that were their only motive, the PLO understands that they cannot prevent a diplomatic settlement of the conflict. They know well that it is to their advantage to take an active part in such a settlement in order to achieve a state of their own. The majority of the guerrilla groups are now in favor of accepting "any land" that can be "wrested from Zionist occupation," rather than continuing to hold back until all of the old Palestine can be recovered. This is a momentous breakthrough. It is true that their statements are qualified and tactical, but then, even accepting a state on the West Bank represents a compromise for them.

All the Arab states officially recognized the PLO at the Algiers summit meeting in November 1973. Only Hussein, who has a vested interest in opposing a secession of the West Bank, did not. However, Hussein's position may be changing since the recent pressures upon him to do so. Prominent Arabs, both in Jerusalem and on the West Bank, have been making overtures to establish ties with the PLO, even though some of them fear for their own positions should the PLO take over. Surely it is to your interest to do the same.

Elon: It is not a question of the PLO accepting any land they can wrest from Zionist occupation, but of whether they will be content with what they will be able to wrest. Will they be ready to live in peace with us, to recognize our national sovereignty and territorial integrity even as we recognize theirs? Are they prepared to have the West Bank demilitarized, so that artillery pieces will not be emplaced ten miles from Tel Aviv? And what does the PLO mean, Sana, by "continuing the struggle by other means"? Do you expect us to hand them a bridgehead from which they may later try to "wrest from Zionist occupation" the rest of the country?

Hassan: Whatever the motives of the present leadership, the situation would completely change if the Palestinians could be pulled out of their present despair. The establishment of a viable Palestinian state, with Israeli and Arab financial help, could take the wind out of the extremists' sails. Furthermore, there is nothing like the trappings of legitimacy to make conservatives of former radicals.

A prosperous, stable Palestinian state may lure the large number of highly educated Palestinians from Jordan, Lebanon and the rest of the Arab world, as well as many of the ambitious young men who are now active in the guerrilla movement. They would be eager to form an elite in their own country.

You must help the PLO save face by giving the West Bank and Gaza back to them, instead of to Hussein. In that way, they would be able to show their people that they have achieved at least some of the national aim. It may enable them to drop a more hard-line position demanding all of Palestine. In the same sense, if you return to them the West Bank and Gaza, rather than their having to wrest it from Hussein, they will be obliged to reciprocate toward you in terms of concessions.

Elon: Well, maybe. But these are long-range prospects. In the short run, the decisive questions remain. Is that Palestinian state on the West Bank going to live in peace with us? Will it agree to your own suggestion, Sana, that the West Bank be demilitarized?

Hassan: Yes, it will live at peace with you. Any representatives of the Palestinian resistance movement who participate in peace talks will have to commit themselves along with the other Arab nations to signing a peace settlement which would grant Israel de jure recognition in exchange for a return of their territories. I believe that the Palestinians will accept demilitarization initially, as a first step, until there is full normalization of relations between you. In the long run, there will be no need for you to insist on demilitarization, since in the context of a genuine peace, neither country will threaten the other's security. This will take time, I admit, but I am convinced it will happen.

The geographical realities—that Gaza and the West Bank are not *physically connected*—will force the Palestinians to maintain good relations with Israel. Another reason for good relations will be the inevitable interdependence of the Israeli and Palestinian economies. Interlocked, the two economies will be a positive inducement to peace.

Elon: Aren't you oversimplifying things, Sana? You presuppose Palestinian unity, Arab unity and an Arab leadership with the ability to carry out such a plan.

Hassan: I don't mean to minimize the problems, but it is important that you give the Palestinians a helping hand in order to make possible this kind of a state in the future.

The Palestinians are now divided between a majority, led by Arafat, which favors accepting the West Bank and Gaza, and a hard-line minority, under George Habash, which does not accept this compromise. The followers of Habash prefer the stalemate. They believe it will enable them to eventually realize their main goal—the taking over of all of Palestine. But they, too, will resign themselves to accept the West Bank if you give them encouraging signals.

When Arafat said that the Palestinian position will not be announced until "five minutes before the twelfth hour," he clearly meant that there was no point in dividing the Palestinians along these militant and moderate lines unless it was apparent that a settlement was near. But he also meant that he was asking for encouragement from Israel and America. Arafat must be sure of Israeli and American support for his minimum objective before he can publicly drop his maximum objective. Help the moderate Palestinians in the difficult task of nation building and of liberation from Hussein's yoke!

I cannot promise that in the short run a Palestinian state will not pursue an irredentist policy supported by the fanatics in Libya or Iraq, nor can anyone guarantee that once in power, the PLO would be able to control its own more extremist elements. But in the long run, I am confident that this extremism will peter out. You must take this risk, for the alternatives are even worse. If you grant the West Bank to Hussein, he will not be able to contain the Palestinian guerrilla action that will result. Then, Israel will reoccupy the West Bank "to restore order." If the Arab countries do nothing, we will be right back where we started from with a new Israeli occupation. If the Arabs intervene, it will mean war.

Elon: But you see how difficult this is? You said yourself that you can't be sure how this future Palestinian state will relate toward Israel. Don't you understand that Israel must be sure, or else she jeopardizes her very life? On these precarious grounds, we might find ourselves in the position of the frog in the famous Middle Eastern anecdote.

Hassan: What frog?

Elon: A scorpion wanted to cross a river and asked the frog to ferry him across. "How can I?" said the frog. "You'll sting me and I'll die." "Nonsense," said the scorpion, "if you die, we both drown." On the strength of this convincing argument the frog started to cross the river with the scorpion on its back. Suddenly the scorpion stung the frog. Its dying words were: "Why—why did you do it? Now we both die." "My dear," said the scorpion, drowning. "This is the Middle East . . ." Should we really ferry the Palestinians across? Should we fight *their* war with Hussein, who seems to want peace with Israel?

What you ask is almost impossible. It is difficult enough for a nation like Israel to liberate itself, let alone play a decisive role in the liberation of another people, especially one that has been our deadliest enemy. We are ourselves engaged in nation building against tremendous odds. And now you ask us to help the Palestinians build their own nation—even while the Palestinians are still propagating their intention to massacre us? It seems almost superhuman.

But if what you say is true, and if the Palestinians are really changing, if they are ready to live in peace and accept demilitarization of the Gaza Strip and of the West Bank—well, then it's an entirely different story. And if the Palestinians make this clear, much clearer than it is today—and Arafat should know that it is later than five to twelve, Sana—then I believe Israel should change her position and deal directly with the Palestinian organizations. Let them set up a state wherever and whenever they want to. On both banks of the Jordan or on the West Bank alone, with King Hussein, against King Hussein, or without him. But I don't want to fight the Palestinians' civil war against Hussein. That is their affair.

Hassan: But even if you help set up a Palestinian state on the West Bank, there would still remain some three hundred thousand Palestinian Arabs within Israel proper. In contrast to them, the Palestinians of the West Bank are to be envied. The Israeli Arabs have the worst of all possible worlds.

Elon: The worst of all possible worlds? Why? They enjoy the highest average living standard of all Arabs anywhere in the world, including the oil sheikdoms of the Arabian Peninsula: the highest standard of health, the highest life expectancy, the lowest infant mortality rate.

I don't want to harp on that old theme. I know that economics is not enough, and high living standards are no substitute for a national identity. What's more important is that they live in a democracy. They vote for and

are elected to Parliament. One of them was Deputy
Speaker of the last Knesset; another served as Deputy
Minister for Health. They sit on the bench as judges,
and serve in the police and in the diplomatic service.
They have their own schools. We don't attempt to make
them into Jews, or even into Israelis in the fullest sense
of this word. We recognize that they are Arabs, Arab
Israelis, not Jewish Israelis. And to spare them the agony
of divided loyalties, they are not compelled to serve in
the army like the rest of us, unless they volunteer, as some
do.

I grant you, things are not easy for them, considering
that they *are* Arabs and we are still at war. But I do
think they are somewhat better off than the West Bank
Palestinians, who have been brutally repressed by the
Jordanian regime between 1948 and 1967. Only four
years ago, in 1970, thousands of Palestinians were killed
by King Hussein's Jordanian army.

Hassan: How wonderful you make it sound, but you gloss
over all the injustices which the Arabs within Israel have
suffered at your hand. In the case of the one million
refugees who are now dispersed throughout the world
as a consequence of the establishment of the state of
Israel, one could argue that their tragedy is a clash
between two national movements, not a result of malicious intent. But you compounded the injustice, under
the pretext of security, by seizing the land of those few
Palestinians who remained in Israel. To the tragedy of
the Palestinian refugees outside of Israel you added the
tragedy of those who remained within Israel. Villagers

were expelled from their lands, whole border regions were sealed off to Arabs, who could only enter them with special permits from the military authorities. These permits were often not granted, and since they could not enter their lands, they could not cultivate them. But then the Israeli government confiscated the lands because "they lay fallow."

Elon: Sana, can you deny that there were real security reasons for sealing off the border regions? The war was still going on. It was a total war with infiltrators crossing the borders every night to cause havoc within Israel.

Hassan: Even outside your so-called security regions, the government confiscated land owned by Arab farmers and parceled it out to Jewish colonies. Even those Palestinian Arabs who did not flee Israel during the war but simply sought safety outside their native villages during the war were not allowed to return to those villages. They were classified by the Israeli government as "refugees" within their own country, where their fathers and forefathers had lived for generations.

For years, the Israeli Arabs were kept under a military administration which controlled their lives, put them under arbitrary house arrest and severely restricted their freedom of movement by a system of passes, without which they could not leave their native regions. This system of travel permits was exploited by the ruling Labor party to coerce the Arabs to vote for them by threatening to withhold passes from those who didn't. True, these injustices were mild compared to the killing of thousands of Palestinians by King Hussein, but a big evil does not justify a small one. Hussein's atrocities are not a yardstick for comparison by a people that claims it seeks to establish not just a nation-state but a just society.

Elon: I fully agree that at one point, over twenty years ago, immediately after the first Arab-Israeli war, lands of Israeli Arabs were confiscated under false security pretexts. The Israeli Supreme Court decried this subterfuge when it responded to appeals by Arab landowners and ordered some of these confiscations reversed. On the whole, I agree there were many injustices. In a large number of cases, "security" was a pretext for a totally unjust system of repression, land expropriation, travel restriction, and so forth. I thank God, Sana, that all these repressive measures and restrictions and infringements of civil and property rights were abolished over a decade ago. In the mid-sixties the Israeli government finally gave in to liberal pressure within Israel, after years of petitioning and street demonstrations by its own people. The restrictions are now a thing of the past. They were not reintroduced in the areas occupied by Israel in 1967. As to your saying that the Labor party exploited these restrictions to extract Arab votes—yes, they certainly tried to, but they didn't really succeed. The majority of Arab votes in Israel go not to Labor but to the Israeli Communist party, which is passionately anti-Zionist and openly endorses the goals of Arab nationalism.

Hassan: I, too, thank God that these restrictions are a thing of the past. But there is no doubt that they have left many scars among Israeli Arabs.

Elon: Of course there are scars. The important thing is that we got rid of those policies.

Hassan: Don't think that the fight put up by Israeli liberals and left-wingers on behalf of the Arabs has gone unnoticed in the Arab world. It's the sort of thing that I, for one, find admirable. Many of us in the Arab world take heart from such events and are encouraged to work for peace, from our side. It's also true that your government has done a lot to raise the living standard of Israeli Arabs, but even there, a great deal more effort is called for if the Arabs are not to remain second-class citizens.

The Arabs, as you know, still rank much lower on all social economic scales compared to Jews. There are two areas in particular in which more effort could be exerted —education and employment. Although Arab education has improved since 1948, it still lags far behind Jewish education. There is a need for increased efforts to see Arabs through secondary schools and universities. In the area of employment, Arabs are passed over for most government jobs because they are considered security risks. They also do not get the better-paying white-collar jobs. In 1970, even the Israeli press was up in arms when the rector of Haifa University denied a job to a young Arab graduate of Hebrew University on political grounds. He was well known to be an Arab nationalist.

Elon: You're quite right there. But you know that that storm in the Israeli press and among the academic community was successful. The man ultimately got the job.

Hassan: The Israeli Arabs do not suffer only from govern-

ment discrimination. They come up against the prejudices of individual Israelis who would prefer hiring a
Jew to an Arab unless it is for menial tasks. And this
attitude is not merely a matter of giving jobs "in the
family." Rather, it reflects the prevailing view among
many Israelis that Arabs are simply not fit for anything
but menial jobs.

Elon: We certainly have our share of bigots.

Hassan: As we do. You say that Israeli Arabs live in a democracy. This is true only in a limited sense. Certainly they
enjoy more freedom than Arabs living in any other Arab
state outside of Lebanon. But they are not able to fully
express themselves politically. Those who are elected to
Parliament, as you know, usually come from a list of
so-called friendly Arabs. They are Uncle Toms, rich
notables who are glad to sell out Arab interests in
exchange for personal gain.

Elon: Whatever you think of the quality of these men, can
you imagine a government official in, say, Syria who happens to be Jewish?

Hassan: First, a moment ago, you measured yourself against
the atrocities of Hussein and now you use the Syrians as
a standard for moral political behavior. What irony for a
nation whose aims were to be "a light for the world"!

Elon: I don't use it as a standard. I was merely pointing
out a fact.

Hassan: I ask you to look at how the Israelis react to real
political challenge. Several attempts to form independent

Arab nationalist parties have been squashed by the Israeli government. This is the crux of the problem. The educational and social needs of the Arabs are still administered by Jews, not by Israeli Arabs. No matter what material benefits you grant them, the Israeli Arabs remain wards of the state, not full-fledged citizens. Arabs as Deputy Speakers of the Knesset or as Deputy Ministers of Health are mere tokens.

In Israel, no Arab could ever move beyond the rank of Deputy, to occupy a major Cabinet post or become Prime Minister. The tragedy is that it is not at all clear that the Israelis believe that an Arab should be able to hold such a post.

Elon: In theory, you're wrong, Sana. A great many Israelis would say that an Arab should be Prime Minister. In practice, however, this would not happen, at least not for as long as there is a war.

Hassan: Really, Amos, I seriously doubt that it would ever happen. The problem is more complicated than a mere statement of political policy as to who can grow up to be Prime Minister. Arabs are outside of the national life because Israel is, first of all, a Jewish religious state, a theocracy which discriminates both in practice and in theory against outsiders. How can the Arabs feel at home in a state where Judaism is the official religion? They resent that.

Elon: So do I. I would like to see a separation of state and synagogue in Israel.

Hassan: At the moment, if I came to Israel, I couldn't marry a Jew unless we went through the subterfuge of a marriage contracted abroad. But that's only a small part of the problem. The larger problem is the problem of identity for Israeli Arabs—their sense of alienation, frustration and political impotence—and the Jewish distrust of Arabs, all Arabs. It is because of this that I say that Israeli Arabs have the worst of all possible worlds. You don't trust them and other Arabs have all along regarded the Israeli Arabs as traitors for recognizing the state of Israel and becoming increasingly integrated in it.

Elon: I would still hope that peace would change all that. I know from my own encounters with Israeli Arabs that sense of alienation of which you speak. A week before the 1967 war I visited a good friend of mine, the well-known Israeli Arab writer Atallah Mansur. We were sitting in his house in Nazareth, watching the news on Syrian television. On the screen before us was a mob in Damascus screaming for war. I asked Mansur, point-blank, "Atallah, what do you really wish would happen?"

He said, "I pray for an Israeli victory." I was surprised, for Mansur is a proud Arab nationalist. His criticism of Israel is regularly published in Israel's most distinguished newspaper, *Haaretz.* "You see," he said, "I need an Israeli victory. I know that the withdrawing Israeli troops will shoot me as a fifth columnist, but the advancing Syrian army will hang me as a collaborator with Israel."

A few weeks after the war I ran into Mansur in a Tel Aviv café. "Well, you got what you wanted," I said teasingly. "The Israelis scored a victory."

"Yes," he said bitterly. "I wanted an Israeli victory, but not *such* a victory."

7

The Distant Future

Hassan: Let's end this dialogue by being a little fanciful, Amos, perhaps even a little crazy. Let's see if we share an image of the future. What is your ideal image of the Middle East in another twenty years?

Elon: We both sound a little mad now, with Arabs and Israelis still shooting one another at this very moment. But let's do it, anyway. Perhaps it's the only sane thing to do and all others are the acts of fools rationalizing their madness, smiling and smug in the name of hard-nosed realism . . .

Shall I draw the blueprint of a Utopia, then? We agreed before, Sana, that reconciliation between us will not take the form of a melodramatic falling into each other's arms. But I hope that by 1990 or so the slow and gradual process of reconciliation will have matured enough to permit open borders, diplomatic relations, cultural exchanges and trade between us. Still, I wouldn't like to see too much trade.

Hassan: Why not?

Elon: Wouldn't it be wiser not to have too close contacts right away? Despite the enormous wealth now accumulating in the Arab countries, the gap in technology, in know-how, in mass education may still be considerable in twenty years' time. The past will still be hard enough to stomach for everybody, and I think especially for the Arabs. I wouldn't like to make a difficult situation even more difficult by large-scale Israeli involvement in the Arab economy.

Tourism, yes, the more the better. Cultural exchanges, yes, the more the better. But in trade and finance, it might be best, even twenty years after the establishment of formal peace, to develop more or less separately. I would hate to see a situation where Israeli construction firms or banks or other businesses we are good at, such as airlines or electronic data processing, would corner important chunks of the Arab market. I wonder if it wouldn't be better if we joined the European Common Market and let you develop yourself. It might be best for you, in view of the accumulated fears of so-called Israeli imperialism and expansionism. And it might be best for us, too, to sharpen our wits in competition with the highly developed industrial countries in Europe rather than take advantage of your relative state of underdevelopment.

Hassan: I disagree with you. I think the more contacts and the more interlocking interests that spring up between us, the better. Look at the effects of the open bridges on the Jordan River—the marketing of Palestinian produce in Israel and the employment of Palestinian labor in Israeli industry and agriculture. Look how it helped ease tensions between Israel and Jordan even before a formal peace. I would have no objections to the Israelis owning the Hilton Hotel in Cairo, as long as the Saudis could own the King David Hotel in Jerusalem. Don't forget that we have even more capital than you do, that we can invest in Israel.

Elon: Do you mean to say that you would actually welcome Israeli experts and Israeli technical assistants in the Arab countries?

Hassan: Yes, by all means. I think there is no shame in admitting that there are many things we can learn from you, just as there are different things you can learn from us. I think that we should encourage all kinds of programs of technical and economic cooperation, provided that your experts and our experts can get together and discuss problems in common to the area.

Elon: Well, I do hope you're right. I'm afraid the experience of other countries, with similar disparities and even without such a past burden of hatred and suspicion, doesn't encourage your point of view. Still, I'm glad you feel that way. Let's, therefore, reverse the question. What is your ideal image of the Near East in twenty years from now?

Hassan: I prefer to be more Utopian than you. If we're going to dream a dream, then it might as well be a beautiful one. I see the whole of the area crisscrossed by hundreds of networks of common interest. Israel and the Arab states will form a common market. We will invest our capital in Israel, and Israel will invest her capital in Arab countries. We will study in your universities, and you will study in ours. We will exchange professors, and our experts will meet at colloquia to discuss problems in common to the area.

Above all, we will have open roads, open bridges and will share each other's full facilities. Tourism and cultural exchange will flourish. *Aïda* will be performed in the city of Suez by the Israeli Philharmonic Orchestra with Leonard Bernstein as conductor, and our famous singer Um Kalsoum will give recitals in Tel Aviv.

Elon: She is very popular there, anyway.

Hassan: I don't think it's too far-fetched at all to say that in twenty years' time you will be playing shesh-besh in Cairo, and Hebrew will have become a second language in Beirut. With your well-known craze for travel—I hope that in Israel you will continue to be as restless as Jews have traditionally been and as curious—you will be swarming in the Beirut market places, and Lebanese ski resorts, and in our museums and pyramids. Masses of Arabs will shop in Tel Aviv, visit the kibbutzim, attend your theaters and swim on your beaches.

Elon: Sana, dear, you sound just like an Israeli! Please don't misunderstand me, there's nothing I would wish more. I hope you're right. If you're right, I will go far beyond and say I wish I could see the Middle East progress in our own lifetime, if possible, beyond the confines of nationalism, which has been the gravedigger of Europe in the first half of this century. If we don't watch out, it may be ours as well. I also have a dream. It ties in well with the aspirations of the early Zionist founding fathers. Perhaps it will be given to our sons or grandsons to realize what our grandfathers had so ardently wished. This is my dream.

Hassan: Nationalism means nothing to me, either. I look forward to the day when we can be linked with you in one transnational federation. But for this to happen, Israel will have to develop a new, *distinctive* identity which derives primarily from her experience in Palestine rather than from her Jewishness or European-ness. I'm convinced that in time the Israeli Jews will be Jews in a national sense, not a religious sense. A new Hebrew people will emerge composed of a majority of Jews, but also including Arabs, Druse and Circassians. The Bible will be a historical document attesting to one aspect of an ancient nationhood in Palestine, but it will take its place beside many other historical documents, legends and folklore which will help the Arabs, Kurds and Circassians realize a stable identity of their own.

Culturally, Israel will no longer be a European enclave. The New Israelis, together, will forge a unique and original culture, a mosaic with Jewish and Arab roots.

You will have to learn Arabic and study the life and culture of the area of which you are inevitably a part, just as Arabs will have to learn the Hebrew language and culture.

Elon: Your dream is beautiful and to be longed for. You know, as we approach the end of this dialogue, you are beginning to sound almost like a veteran Zionist idealist, like Theodor Herzl in 1899, or Chaim Weizmann in 1919.

But I am a little surprised that you are addressing yourself to Israel only. Doesn't your dream include Arab countries as well? Don't you think that you would first have to achieve in the Arab countries at least a measure of political tolerance, democracy, freedom of the individual? Most Arab countries today are repressive, bigoted, theocracies with little tolerance, and except for Lebanon, there is no democracy or individual liberties.

Hassan: I agree we still have much to do to improve the Arab countries before we approach the situation in which Israel already is today. If I don't want you to be a European enclave, I can't realistically expect you to be an enclave of angelic creatures within a hostile, intolerant Arab world. But as the Arab world itself modernizes, my dream about Israel may not be as far-fetched as it sounds. The fear of many Israelis that assimiliation in the area would mean "Levantinization" was not caused only by your European antecedents and prejudices which isolated you from the culture and sensibilities of our area. It was also the result of the implacable hostility of the Arabs, our total rejection and boycott of Israel.

All of this will change quite spontaneously once we have peace. You will see, Amos, we will be learning

Hebrew and you Arabic, not just because these are compulsory drudgery courses like gymnastics, but because we are dying to find out more about each other. Berlitz will have so many applicants for Arabic and Hebrew courses that they won't know what to do!

Elon: I am sure this will happen. As we become more assimilated in the area and you become more Europeanized, we shall meet somewhere midway.

Hassan: Once the Palestinians have found their identity and a state of their own, I hope that it will be possible to bring their identity and yours closer together.

Elon: They will have to. We will undoubtedly live with one another. There will always be a sizable Arab minority within Israel,, as there may be a sizable Israel minority within the Palestinian state. Let each have double nationality, if necessary, and vote for both Parliaments. As our identities and cultures converge we will try to be a part of a higher, larger whole, without losing our own particular faces.

Hassan: Let's hope the next stage will be a United States of the Middle East when all barricades between people will have fallen. The old European nations are moving in this direction. I hope that in twenty-five years we shall be moving in that direction too. I know this sounds crazy today, but if it helped to be a little crazy to be a Zionist, maybe it will help us also.

Elon: *Inshalah.*

Hassan: Well, here we are. We agree on some points and we disagree on others. Have we found a reconciling formula?

Elon: Have we? It would be pompous to even consider that *we* might. But I think we more or less managed to do what we set out to do. W. H. Auden once wrote that "private faces in public places are wiser and nicer than public faces in private places"—I'm not sure we can even claim that. But I think we've both discovered, haven't we, that reconciliation begins with mutual compassion?

Hassan: Yes, compassion. We ought to build up as much compassion as possible before the guns cut us short once more.

Elon: By the way, Sana, what kind of reaction do you get from Egyptian government people to the views you hold? Are they angry at you?

Hassan: Some are annoyed but others hold the same view as I do. Some say I am too soft on Israel. One high Egyptian official told me just recently that I was giving away our bargaining position prematurely, before negotiations have begun.

Elon: That's funny. I have had that kind of criticism from some of our officials too.

Hassan: This is the time for those of us Arabs who disagree with our governments to say so.

Elon: And for Israelis, too.

About the Authors

AMOS ELON was two years old when his parents migrated from Vienna to British-mandated Palestine in 1930. He was an infantryman during the 1948 and 1956 wars, and a war correspondent during the 1967 fighting. Besides *The Israelis: Founders and Sons,* he is the author of a study of postwar Germany, *Journey Through a Haunted Land,* and of numerous articles. He lives in Israel and in Italy.

SANA HASSAN is a young scholar and writer whose articles and reviews have appeared in prominent magazines and newspapers. She is now at work on her second book, *Israel Through Egyptian Eyes,* a diary of her travels in Israel. She is the daughter of Mahmoud Hassan Pasha, one-time Egyptian Ambassador to the United States and to the United Nations. Ms. Hassan is married to a high official in the Egyptian government. She currently lives in Cambridge, Massachusetts, and in Cairo.